To Sagelquist
Hope you enjoy the book
Robert E Hollmann
April 22, 2006
San Jacinto

Frontier Legends

presents

Jim Bowie

by

Robert E. Hollmann

Printed in the United States of America.

For information address:
Durban House Publishing Company, Inc.
7502 Greenville Avenue, Suite 500, Dallas, Texas 75231

Library of Congress Cataloging-in-Publication Data
Hollmann, Robert E., 1944 -

Jim Bowie / Robert E. Hollmann

Library of Congress Control Number: 2005935729
p. cm.

ISBN 1-930754-81-7
First Edition

10 9 8 7 6 5 4 3 2 1

Visit our Web site at
http://www.durbanhouse.com

To Biscuit

A Good Dog

Acknowledgements

Many people gave invaluable assistance in the writing of this book. I want to thank Eric Sanchez and Naomi Chapman, two students, who read the transcript and provided insight into what works for young readers. I want to thank Tammie Sanchez and Linda Pierce for their suggestions and comments. I want to thank Ben Ellison of Benjamin's photography for the book picture. Thanks to my two good friends, Mignon Johnson and Freda Redd, for their encouragement and interest. As usual I want to thank my daughters, Kristina and Kasey, and my son, Rob, for their support. Also thanks to my wife, Kathy, for all you do.

Robert E. Hollmann
Odessa, Texas
August 2005

Jim Bowie

Chapter One

THE OLD DOG WANDERED SLOWLY across the yard to the little cabin. The hard-packed dirt of the front yard hurt his paws. The noonday sun was hot and the old dog was looking for a cool place to lie down. Stopping in front of a half filled bowl of water, he lapped up some. He looked at an old bone that lay next to the bowl, but there was no meat on it, so he walked on. He walked around the corner of the house and found a shady spot. The old dog stretched and lay down with his head on his paws. He yawned once and was soon asleep.

"Grampa. Wake up."

The sudden noise startled the old dog and he jerked his head up. He yawned again as he searched for the source of the noise that had woken him up. Two small puppies were racing toward him. Their ears flapped and their tongues hung from the sides of their mouths as they ran. The old dog put his head back on his paws and closed his eyes.

He felt the small dogs come to a stop beside him. He heard them panting. Finally one of them said, "Get up, Grampa. We want to play with you."

Slowly the old dog opened his eyes and looked at the puppies.

"Go away. It's too hot to play. Besides, I'm tired."

The girl puppy walked over and licked the old dog's face.

"Please, Grampa. We like to play with you."

The old dog stretched and slowly stood up.

"Now, Princess, I like to play with you and Butch too. But it's too hot right now. We would all get sick playing in this hot sun."

Butch jumped at a passing butterfly and then sat next to the old dog.

"Well, there's nothing to do. Daddy is out hunting and Momma is watching the sheep. We want to do something."

The old dog found a softer spot and lay down again.

"You can take a nap with me."

"No. We don't want to take a nap," both puppies howled at once.

"Well, I do. Now don't bother me." The old dog closed his eyes.

Princess walked over and lay down beside him.

"At least tell us a story."

Butch ran over and plopped down next to Princess.

"Yeah. Tell us the one about when you were young and were friends with that big man."

The old dog opened one eye.

"Big man? Oh, you must mean Jim Bowie. Why, I've told you that story a hundred times, don't you want to hear something else?"

"No." Both puppies shook their heads. "We want to hear that one."

The old dog sat up and scratched his ear with his hind foot.

"Well, now, let's see. That was a long time ago. I was no bigger than you are now. I was living in Louisiana. My parents had both died and I was all by myself in the swamps. It was hard to stay alive then. There was not much food that I could catch, and there were a lot of things that wanted to catch me."

Both of the puppies sat up and watched the old dog. He looked far away looking at something from long ago.

"I was walking through the swamps one day and I heard voices. Back then I didn't know what humans were, so I hid in a bush by the riverbank. Pretty soon I saw two young men walking through the trees. They had a net and some rope and I could hear them talking. I was scared because I didn't know what they were going to do. I lay down as low as I could under that bush and watched them walk by. They stopped right next to my bush and I heard them talking..."

"Jim, you're crazy to want to try and wrestle an alligator. Ma is going to skin you if she finds out."

"Well, Rezin, she won't know if you don't tell her. I think it's fun to wrestle an alligator. Now, let's go find one."

"I watched the two men walk away. They seemed like they were pretty nice. I decided to go after them and see what happened. I stood up and started to follow the men when I heard a sound behind me. I turned and saw a big alligator with his mouth wide open… coming right for me."

Chapter Two

THE OLD DOG LAID HIS HEAD BACK ON HIS PAWS and closed his eyes.

"Grandpa," Princess called out. "Wake up. Tell us the rest of the story."

The old dog opened his eyes and yawned. He looked at the two puppies watching him with wide eyes.

"Oh, all right. Now where was I? Oh, yes. The alligator was coming right for me. I turned and tried to run up the bank, but it was wet and I slipped down toward the alligator. I turned to run again and I felt the alligator bite down on my tail. I yelped and tried to pull away, but the alligator was too strong. I felt myself being pulled toward the alligator and there was nothing I could do about it. I knew I was a goner."

The old dog shivered as he thought about being food for the alligator. "Just when I had given up all hope, I heard something crashing through the bushes. I looked up and saw the young man called Jim leap off the riverbank with a yell. He flew over me and landed on the alligator's back. The alligator was surprised and opened his mouth. I jumped away, but part of my tail fell off. I ran under the bush where I had been hiding and watched as Jim sat on the alligator's back and grabbed the alligator's jaws, holding his mouth shut. Jim was yelling and holding on as tightly as he could, while the alligator moved his body from side to side, trying to throw Jim off his back."

Princess snuggled up to the old dog while Butch stood up and said, "If I had been there, I would have grabbed that alligator's tail and bitten it clean off. That's what I would have done."

The old dog shook his head and continued his story.

"Jim was holding on for dear life, and I could tell that the alligator was getting tired. I looked up and saw Jim's brother, Rezin, looking down at the fight…"

"Hold on, Jim. I think he's giving up."

Jim's face was turning red and he was breathing hard, but he held on to the alligator's jaws. The movement of the gator's tail was getting slower and slower. All at once, Jim hopped off the alligator and turned him over on his back. Jim began to rub the gator's stomach and soon the alligator was asleep. Jim slowly stood up and smiled at his brother.

"Wow, that sure was fun. That gator was strong. I was worried there for a little while."

Rezin walked down next to Jim. "You better be worried. That gator tore your shirt. Remember what Ma told you? Don't be wrestling alligators and don't be tearing up your clothes. You're going to be in more trouble with her than you were with that alligator."

Jim looked at the rip in his shirt and shrugged.

"I'll tell her I caught it on a tree. She can't get mad about that."

"Jim, you can't lie to Ma. She sees right through you every time. Well, we best be getting back home. I think that alligator will be waking up pretty soon."

Rezin walked up the riverbank. Jim looked over at the bush where I was hiding.

"Hold on, Rezin."

Jim walked over to the bush and knelt down to look at me. He held out his hand.

"Come here, pup," he said.

I backed further under the bush and growled, trying to sound mean. Jim smiled and reached into his pocket. He pulled out a piece of meat and held it toward me.

"Are you hungry?" he asked. "Wrestling alligators always makes me hungry."

I sniffed at the meat. It had been a while since I had eaten. It smelled good. I looked at Jim. He seemed friendly. I took a step forward and licked the meat. It tasted good. I took the meat from Jim's hand and began to chew it. It sure tasted good. Jim rubbed his hand on my head while I ate. When I was finished I licked his hand to let him know he was my friend. Jim felt my tail where the alligator had bitten it.

"You're sure lucky, pup. That alligator wanted you for supper."

"Come on, Jim," Rezin called. "We have to get home. Ma will be mad enough about your shirt without us being late for supper."

Jim picked me up and rubbed my head. I snuggled against him. I felt safe for the first time in a long while.

"You taking that pup home?" Rezin asked.

Jim nodded.

"I can't leave him out here to be alligator food. He looks like a good pup. He could stand some good food, and Ma's the best cook around."

I watched Rezin shake his head.

"You're always picking up strays, Jim. What are you going to call him?"

Jim looked at the alligator that was beginning to stir. He reached down and felt the stump of my tail where the alligator had bitten it.

"I think I'll call him Gator. Let's go. Ma will have supper waiting."

Chapter Three

As Jim carried me through the swamps I began to relax. Soon I fell asleep and did not wake up until I heard Rezin call out.

"Hello. We're home. Is supper ready?"

I looked up and saw a small cabin sitting in the center of a clearing. Smoke drifted from the chimney and a small woman stood in the doorway watching us. She waved then walked back into the house. Jim carried me inside the cabin.

"Hey, Ma. We got something for this dog to eat?"

I watched the old lady as she looked me over.

"Where did you get this mutt? He looks like gator food."

Jim laughed. "He nearly was. See his tail? A gator bit it off. I reckon he just needs some good food and he'll make a fine-looking dog."

The old lady shook her head as she put some meat scraps in front of me. "I swear, Jim Bowie. You're always bringing home strays. Well, go wash up. Supper's ready. Then take off your shirt so I can mend it. I guess you've been wrestling alligators again."

THE NEXT FEW YEARS were some of the happiest of my life. Jim and I roamed the swamps together. He grew into a strong man and I grew into a pretty good dog, if I do say so myself. We had a lot of fun. Jim wrestled alligators from time to time and we hunted and fished and spent our time outdoors. Sometimes Rezin would come with us, but mostly it was me and Jim.

There was one man who didn't like Jim. He was the local sheriff who also served as a banker. One day Jim and I walked into his office.

"Hello, Norris," Jim said. "I need to talk to you."

"Have a seat." He motioned to a chair. "What can I do for you?"

"Well you see, I need a loan. I have a chance to do some business, but I need some money to get the business started."

The banker leaned back in his chair. "I don't think I can help you. I know some of the people you do business with, like that pirate, Jean Lafitte. I don't think it would be smart for me to loan you money."

Jim leaned forward in his chair. "Now, look here, Norris. Mr. Lafitte is not involved in this business, and even if he were, as long as I pay you back, why do you care who is in it?"

"I care because it's my money, and I don't have to give it to somebody if I don't want to. I think you need to take your mangy dog and get out of my office."

Jim stood up. "Now look here, Norris. Just because you don't like me doesn't mean you can talk bad about my dog."

Jim took a step toward the banker. Norris reached into his desk and pulled out a pistol. He fired it at Jim, but Jim ducked and the ball hit the wall. Jim looked at the banker through the curling smoke.

"I'll go. But I won't forget this."

I followed him out of the office. We walked down the street and saw Rezin walking toward us. He had a package under his arm.

"What's the shooting all about?" he asked.

Jim looked back at the office where Norris was peeking out of a window.

"I asked Norris for a loan and he didn't want to give it to me. He insulted Gator, and when I stood up he shot at me. I didn't have a weapon, so I left. I reckon I'll see him again sometime."

Rezin handed the package to Jim.

"I think you might need this. I had it made especially for you."

Jim took the package and unwrapped it. Inside was the biggest knife I had ever seen. The blade was long and curved at the end. It had a sharp point for stabbing, but it also had a sharp edge for cutting. The hand guard covered Jim's big hand. The upper edge was wide enough to block the thrust of another knife. Jim held the knife and swung it in a circle.

"There is some weight to this. This is the best knife I have ever seen. Where did you get it?"

"I had the blacksmith make it. With all the fights you're getting into lately, I decided you needed some way to protect yourself."

Jim took the scabbard from Rezin and slipped the knife into it.

"Thanks, Rezin. I appreciate this."

Rezin walked over and put his arm around Jim's shoulder.

"Jim, I think it would be a good idea for you to get out of here for awhile. You have some pretty strong enemies. Norris is the sheriff, and he could make it really hard on you."

Jim thought about what Rezin had said.

"You could be right, but I don't know where I would go."

"Jim, there's a place where land is free for the taking. Where you can hunt and fish as much as you like. I even heard there are gold mines there."

"Really? Where is this place?"

"Texas. I hear that you can do whatever you want there and nobody will bother you."

Jim reached down and scratched my ears.

"Texas. That's part of Mexico. I hear that the Mexican government doesn't want people coming in and taking land without permission."

"Well, it's not hard to get permission. They want settlers. And a man like you could do well there. You could make a fortune."

"How about you, Rezin? You coming with me?"

Rezin shook his head. "Jim, I can't leave Ma right now. You know she's getting old. I need to look after her. But you get settled and get a big place, then send for us. We'll come live with you."

Jim stared into the distance. He appeared to be trying to see Texas.

"You make it seem real tempting, Rezin."

"You need to give it a try, Jim. You don't have anything to lose and a whole lot to gain. Besides, if you stay here you're going to end up in jail, or dead."

Jim straightened up. He looked at the knife that Rezin had given him. He glanced back at the office where Norris still watched him from the window. He looked down at me and smiled.

"Well, Gator. It looks like you and me are going to Texas."

Chapter Four

"Ow! BUTCH, LET GO OF MY EAR!" Princess yelped.

The old dog looked up to see Butch pulling on one of Princess' ears with his teeth.

"Here, Butch. Stop that right now," Gator said. "What's wrong with you?"

Butch dropped the ear and hung his head.

"I want to sit next to you. She always gets to sit next to you."

The old dog shook his head. "If you two are going to fight, I'm going to take a nap." He stretched out in the shade.

"No, Grampa," Butch said. "We'll be good. Tell us the story."

Princess curled up next to the old dog. "Yes, Grampa. We want to hear the story."

The old dog raised his head. "Well, all right. But any more fighting and that's the end of the story."

Butch lay down next to Princess. The old dog scratched his ear with a hind foot.

"Now, where was I? Oh, yes. Jim and I headed for Texas. I tell you I had no idea how big Texas was. We walked for days. The grass on the prairie came up to the belly of Jim's horse. Most of the time it was over my head. Sometimes we would flush a rabbit and I would chase him, but those Texas rabbits are fast. I never caught one. Along the trail we met up with a man named Isaac Donoho. He and Jim became friends and he rode with us.

One evening just about sunset, we saw a campfire glowing in the distance. We headed toward the fire and came upon three men cooking supper. The cooking meat sure smelled good. As we got near the camp Jim called out, "Hello. We'd like to come into your camp."

The men reached for their rifles, and Jim and Isaac held out their hands to show they were friendly.

"Hold it right there," one of the men around the campfire said.

"It's all right, friend," Jim said. "We're traveling through Texas and would like to spend the night here if you don't mind. This is Isaac Donoho. My name is Jim Bowie."

The men looked at each other. The one who had spoken walked up to Jim and said. "Jim Bowie? The knife fighter? I heard of him. If you are really Jim Bowie, let me see that knife."

Jim smiled and slowly pulled his knife from the scabbard. He turned it so the handle was pointing toward the man and handed it to him.

"Here you go. Be careful. It's mighty sharp."

The man took the knife and held it carefully. He turned to his friends.

"I've never seen a knife like this. I think this is the best knife I've ever seen. I guess you really are Jim Bowie. You and your friend are welcome to have some supper and stay here tonight."

"Thank you," Jim said as he stepped down from his horse. "That food smells mighty good."

"We found a small herd of buffalo. Nothing better than roast buffalo." The man walked over and sat by the fire. "My name's Turner. This here is Johnson and Smith. We're headed to San Felipe. We're going to see Mr. Austin."

"Stephen F. Austin?" Jim asked.

Turner nodded. "The very same. He's the man to see about getting some land grants. There's a lot of land available in Texas."

Jim poured himself a cup of coffee. "Sure is. We've been riding for days and it looks like we'll be riding for several more days."

Turner cut a slice of meat from the roasting buffalo. "Where are you heading?"

Jim blew on the hot coffee. "No place special. We're just looking over the country. We want to get some land and we're searching for a good spot."

Turner took a bite of the meat. "Why don't you ride with us to meet Austin? He knows where all the best land is. He could probably help you get a grant. He's in good with the government of Mexico."

Jim looked over at his friend. "What do you think, Isaac? Should we go meet Mr. Austin?"

Isaac shrugged. "I don't think it could hurt anything. We don't really have any plans. He might get us lined up with some good land."

Jim took a sip of the coffee. "All right then, Turner. We'll ride with you to see Mr. Austin. Now if you don't mind, I think I'll try some of that buffalo."

Jim pulled his knife and cut a large slice of the roasting meat. The fat dripped into the fire and sent sparks dancing in the dark sky. The smell of the meat was wonderful. I was hungry. I looked around at the men, but they were eating and talking. It was plain that no one was going to give me anything to eat. I walked over to the meat and stuck out my tongue. I licked the meat. It sure tasted good. Just then the fire sparked and some sparks landed on my tongue. I yelped and ran away from the fire looking for some water to cool my tongue. As I ran into the darkness I could here Jim and the others laughing. I found a small puddle of water and lapped it with my burning tongue.

As the cool water poured over my tongue I heard Jim say, "I think old Gator's going to think he's better off with an alligator chasing him than a fire burning his tongue."

The men were still laughing as I slunk back toward the camp. I was determined to get some of that meat, and this time I would watch out for the fire.

Chapter
Five

I TROTTED ALONGSIDE THE HORSES as they walked down the dusty street of San Felipe. The town didn't look like much. There were a few wooden buildings lining the dirt street. A dog came running at me, barking and showing his teeth. Jim swerved his horse toward the dog and it ran away. Jim looked down at me and smiled.

"You sure have a way of making friends fast, Gator."

I looked up at Jim and wagged my tail. He was always looking after me, but someday I was going to show him that I could take care of myself.

"Which building is Austin in, Turner?" Jim asked.

Turner took off his hat and scratched his head.

"I'm not sure." He saw a woman walking down the

street and called to her. "Excuse me, Ma'am. Do you know where I might find Mr. Stephen Austin?"

The woman studied the men for a few moments. Then she pointed to a building at the end of the street.

"He's in there," she said.

"Many thanks," Turner said as he replaced his hat. The men rode down the street and tied their horses in front of the building. I followed the men through the door. There was a small desk in the room, and a man was busy writing at the desk. He looked up as we entered the room.

"What can I do for you fellows?" he asked.

Jim walked over to him and extended his hand.

"Would you be Mr. Stephen Austin?"

The man took Jim's hand. "I would."

"My name's Jim Bowie. My friends and I would like a word with you if you have the time."

Austin stood up.

"Jim Bowie. I've heard of you, sir. Your reputation and that knife of yours are well known around here. We've heard about the fight you had at the Sandbar.

I wonder if you would let me see your knife?"

Jim took his knife from its scabbard and handed it to Austin. Austin waved it through the air a few times and then handed it back to Jim.

"A truly amazing knife." Austin sat down. "Now what can I do for you gentlemen?"

Jim sat in a chair across from Austin. I walked over and lay down in a corner of the room. The other men stood near the doorway.

"Well, Mr. Austin." Jim looked back at his friends.

"We were wanting to find a good place to set up a home. We thought you might be able to tell us where we could find some good land. "

Austin rubbed his chin.

"Well, land is not as easy to find as it used to be. There's some trouble with the government of Mexico. I think they're getting worried about all the new settlers coming to Texas from the United States. They're not as willing to give out grants as they once were."

Austin searched the papers on his desk. He pulled out a clean sheet and began to write. For several moments there was no sound in the room except the scratching of the pen on the paper. Austin finished his writing and looked up at Jim.

"This is a letter that will introduce you to two very important men in San Antonio. Mr. Juan De Veramendi and Mr. Juan Seguin. Mr. Seguin's father, Don Erasmo Seguin, is a strong supporter of the new settlers. I think these men can help you find some good land."

Jim took the paper from Austin.

"Thank you, sir. You said that the government of Mexico wasn't happy with the new settlers. Do you expect trouble?"

Austin leaned back in his chair and sighed.

"I'm afraid that there will be. There are some people here who want us to separate from Mexico. These men are causing trouble and I'm afraid that Mexico will send an army to stop the troublemakers."

"You don't want to separate from Mexico?" Jim asked.

"I don't think we could win a war with Mexico.

They're too strong and we're not organized. Too many people want to be the leaders. One of the worst is a young man from South Carolina named William Travis. He and his friends stir up trouble whenever they can. It's not good for Texas."

Jim stood up. "Well, Mr. Austin. I didn't come to Texas to get in a fight. I just want to find a place and settle down. Thank you for your letter. I guess we'll go find these men."

Austin stood up and shook Jim's hand.

"Well, if trouble does come, I'm glad to know we have Jim Bowie on our side."

I followed Jim and the others outside. They mounted their horses and rode out of town. Turner rode up beside Jim.

"What do you think about the trouble with Mexico?"

Jim looked out across the open prairie.

"I don't know right now. Maybe these two gentlemen will know more. One thing I do know: if the Mexican government starts trouble, I'll sic ol' Gator on 'em."

Chapter
Six

THE STREETS OF SAN ANTONIO WERE ALIVE with activity
as we searched for the home of Juan Veramendi. I had to
dodge horses and wagons as we rode down the street. Jim
saw a man he knew and called to him.

"Hey, Ben. I thought they'd have run you out of
Texas by now."

The man smiled as he walked over to Jim. He shook
Jim's hand.

"Now, why would they want to do that? It's been a
while since I've seen you, Jim. Heard a lot about you. I
think your knife is more famous than you are."

Jim turned to his friends.

"This is Ben Milam. I've known him for some time."

Jim looked down the street. "Ben, can you tell us where Juan Veramendi lives? Stephen Austin told us to look him up. We also need to find a man named Juan Seguin."

"Well, you're in luck. Both of those gentlemen are at the Veramendi house right now. I just left them." Milam looked around the street to make sure no one was listening. "I'm glad you're here, Jim. I think there's trouble coming, and we can use a man like you."

"I didn't come here to get in a fight, Ben. I could have stayed home and had all the fighting I wanted. We're interested in finding some land and starting a ranch."

I walked over to Milam. He reached down and scratched my ears.

"This mutt yours?" he asked.

Jim nodded. "His name's Gator. I don't think he's good for much except alligator bait."

I licked Milam's hand. He looked down at my face.

"Jim, I don't believe you. If you thought that, you wouldn't let him follow you all over Texas."

"Well, do you know where the Veramendi house is?"

Milam nodded.

"Go down the street to the church. Take the street to the right. It's the big house on the corner. When you get through there, come find me and we'll talk about old times."

Jim turned his horse in the direction indicated by Milam.

"Thanks, Ben. I'll find you later."

Shortly Jim tied his horse in front of a large house and walked up to the front door. I stood beside him as he knocked. Soon a servant opened the door and asked what

Jim wanted. Jim pulled the letter from Austin out of his pocket.

"I have a letter from Mr. Stephen Austin, introducing me to Mr. Juan Veramendi. I heard that Mr. Juan Seguin was here. I was hoping to speak with him too."

The servant took the letter and walked back into the house. Shortly he came back and said, "Mr. Veramendi will see you."

Jim turned to his friends. "Go find us a place to stay. I'll meet you at the cantina later."

Nobody stopped me, so I followed Jim into the house. The thick adobe walls made it cool inside. We followed the servant into a large room. Two men were sitting around a big table talking. The men got to their feet as we entered the room. The servant bowed to the men and said. "This is Mr. Jim Bowie."

The servant left the room as the two men walked over to Jim and shook his hand.

"Mr. Bowie. Welcome to my home. I am Juan Veramendi, and this is Juan Seguin."

"Just call me Jim. Thanks for seeing me, Mr. Veramendi."

"What can we do for you, Jim?"

The men sat down around the table.

"My friends and I are looking for some good land to start a ranch. Mr. Austin said you might be able to help us find that land."

"There's some very nice land in Texas." Veramendi looked at Juan Seguin. "But, I'm afraid that there's a problem with the government in Mexico. They're worried about all the settlers from the United States coming to

Texas. They think that the settlers want to take Texas away from Mexico and join the United States. They're not willing to give land to new settlers because of this."

Jim sat back in his chair.

"Mr. Veramendi, I didn't come to take Texas away from anybody. I only want a chance to start a new life."

Veramendi smiled. "I understand. I didn't mean that you couldn't get some land. Only that it will take some work."

Just then a small dog came running into the room. He was barking and showing his teeth to me. I jumped up from where I was lying and charged at the dog. He turned and ran yelping toward the door. Suddenly a woman stepped into the doorway and picked up the dog. I stopped at her feet.

"Chico. You should not be coming into this room while these men are talking."

I looked at her face and then back at Jim. I could tell he thought the same thing that I did. This was the most beautiful woman we had ever seen.

Chapter Seven

"WHO WAS THE BEAUTIFUL WOMAN?" Princess asked.

"Be quiet and let him tell the story," Butch told her.

"Make me," Princess said.

Butch jumped on her and they rolled across the yard, barking and nipping at each other's ears.

"You two go fight somewhere else. I'm going to take a nap."

The old dog turned away from the puppies. They came running toward him with their tongues hanging out and their ears blowing in the breeze. They skidded to a stop beside the old dog.

"No. Go on with the story. We'll be good."

The old dog looked off into the distance.

"I remember it like it was happening now. The lady stood there holding that yapping dog and looking at Jim and me. She smiled and the whole room seemed to light up. Mr. Veramendi walked over to her…"

"Ursula. This is Mr. Jim Bowie. Mr. Bowie this is my daughter, Ursula."

Jim stood and bowed.

"It is a pleasure to meet you, Miss Veramendi."

"Thank you. Please call me Ursula."

She looked down at me and patted my head.

"Is this your dog?"

Jim nodded. "Yes. His name is Gator."

She held her little dog down next to my face, and he snapped at me. I jumped back and growled. Jim walked over and grabbed me by the skin of my neck. He pulled me away.

"Gator. You go outside. Right now."

I hung my head and started to walk toward the door.

"No. Mr. Bowie, please. It was Chico's fault. Gator did nothing wrong." Two other women walked into the room. Ursula handed her dog to one of them and walked over to me. She knelt down and rubbed my head between my ears. I wagged my tail and licked her hand. Her hand was soft and it felt good on my head.

Mr. Veramendi pointed to the other women.

"Mr. Bowie. These are my other daughters, Juana and Gertrudis." Jim nodded to the women. Ursula stood up. She took her dog from Juana, then turned to Jim.

"Tonight there's a party in the town square. You should come. It'll be fun."

"Thank you. I'll tell my friends. They'd probably like to go to a party after so many nights camping out on the trail."

The ladies left and the men sat back at the table.

Juan Seguin looked at Jim. "I think you'll like it in Texas. There are many opportunities here."

"I think I'll like it here too," Jim said as he looked at the door where the ladies had gone. "All I want is an opportunity. If you'll help me, I think we will all be happy."

Mr. Veramendi stood. "Juan, take Jim and show him and his friends where they can stay. Jim, I think you should come to the party tonight. We'll have a chance to visit about some plans I have."

Soon Jim, Juan Seguin and I were walking into the cantina. We saw our friends sitting at a table and we walked over to them.

"Howdy, Jim," Turner said. "We couldn't find a place to stay so we came on in here."

Jim and Juan sat down and I curled up at Jim's feet.

"That's all right. Juan will show us where we can stay. You boys need to clean up. We've been invited to a party tonight."

"That sounds good to me," Turner said. "I hope they have some good food. I'm tired of eating the food we had on the trail. Good home cooking would sure hit the spot."

"There will be plenty of food," Juan said. "There will be many people there. It'll be good for you to meet them."

"We look forward to it, Juan," Jim said. "Come on, boys. Juan is going to get us a place to stay."

The men got up to follow Juan. I watched Jim. I could tell he was thinking about what Mr. Veramendi was going to talk to him about. I could also tell he was thinking about Mr. Veramendi's daughter.

Chapter Eight

IT WAS A BEAUTIFUL NIGHT. The moon was full and the stars filled the skies. The plaza was crowded with people, and the sounds of guitars and fiddles floated through the air. The smell of food cooking made my mouth water. Jim and I walked through the crowd of people. We saw Mr. Veramendi sitting at a table, and we walked over to him. Mr. Veramendi smiled as he saw us standing there.

"Jim. I'm glad you came. Please sit down."

Jim sat down across from Mr. Veramendi. I started to lie at his feet, but the smell of the food made me walk around to different tables. At each table I would sit and stare at the people sitting there. I would look as hungry as I could until someone would hand me a piece of meat.

The food tasted as good as it smelled, and soon I was too full to eat anymore. I walked back over to Jim and curled up under the table next to Jim's feet.

I heard Jim talking to Mr. Veramendi.

"You said you had some plans. Would you mind telling me what they are?"

Mr. Veramendi chuckled. "Not at all. Because I think you can be a part of them. I think it's fortunate that you came to San Antonio. I'm aware of your reputation. You're the kind of man I need."

Jim leaned forward in his chair. I could tell he was very interested in what Mr. Veramendi was going to say.

"Jim. I am going to be appointed vice-governor of the province of Texas and Coahuila. That will give me a great deal of influence. I'll be able to see you get all the land you want. But, Jim, there's a greater plan. A plan that will make us very rich."

Jim sat back in his chair. "I like the sound of the word 'rich.' What's your plan?"

Mr. Veramendi looked around to make sure that no one was listening.

"There's a story that I've heard for many years. West of San Antonio there's an old mission called Santa Cruz de San Saba. Not far from there, there's said to be a mine. In the mine it is said there's a fortune in silver. Enough to make many men rich."

"How does this involve me?" Jim asked.

"I can't go look for the mine. I need a man I can trust. A man who is not afraid to go to that area and search for the mine."

"What's there to be afraid of? Are there ghosts

guarding the mine?"

Mr. Veramendi shook his head.

"Not that I know of. There's something much worse. Comanche Indians roam that area. Have you heard of the Comanche?"

Jim shook his head. "No."

"Jim, these are the most warlike Indians we have in Texas. They ride their horses like they are part of the animals. They have no fear. And they do not like anyone coming into their territory. The mission there is abandoned, and the Comanches are the reason."

"What do you want me to do?"

"I want you to take some men to San Saba and find the mine. I'll see you have the supplies you need. We can be partners."

"When do you want me to go?"

"It won't be for a while. I'll be appointed vice-governor next week. I'll see you have your land. We need to plan your search carefully. If word of this search gets out, there'll be many people looking for the mine. I want you to pick your men carefully. Be sure you can trust them."

Jim looked over to the table where his friends were sitting. "I can trust those men. I think I'll ask my brother, Rezin, to come too."

Mr. Veramendi shook Jim's hand. "We'll talk about this some more later. Now enjoy the party."

Ursula walked over to the table and sat down. Mr. Veramendi smiled at her.

"Are you having a good time, Daughter?"

"It's a nice party." She looked at Jim. "Most of these men cannot dance. They stomp around and yell and think they're dancing."

Jim smiled at her. "I'm afraid I would be one of those men. I never learned to dance in the swamps."

"Where are your sisters?" Mr. Veramendi asked.

"Gertrudis is dancing. She doesn't mind the stomp-ing and yelling. Juana is talking to Dr. Alsbury. I think she likes him."

Mr. Veramendi looked over at Juana and Dr. Alsbury.

"He seems like a nice man. I don't mind Juana talking to him." Mr. Veramendi stood up. "I must say good night. I have much to do tomorrow. Please stop by tomorrow, Jim. We can talk some more."

Jim watched Mr. Veramendi walk away. He turned to Ursula.

"Well, Ursula. If you can stand some stomping and yelling, I'd like to dance with you."

Ursula held out her hand.

"It would be my pleasure, Jim."

Hours later, after the party had ended, Jim and I walked along the banks of the San Antonio river. It was quiet and Jim did not talk as we walked along. I could tell he was thinking. A fish jumped in the river and I watched the ripples as they widened and then disappeared. Jim reached down and scratched my ears.

"Let's go get some sleep, Gator. I need to see Mr. Veramendi tomorrow. I think we're going to be glad we came to Texas."

Chapter
Nine

THE NEXT YEAR FLEW BY. Jim and Mr. Veramendi spent a lot of time together discussing land deals and planning the search for the lost mines near San Saba. Jim also spent a lot of time with Ursula. They went for walks by the river and rode to the nearby prairies for picnics. I enjoyed these outings. Ursula was always nice to me. On the picnics she always brought me a special treat. I had fun chasing rabbits on the prairies, although I never caught one.

One day I was chasing a rabbit in some tall grass. I heard the grass rustling to my right. I bounded through the grass and came face to face with a large rattlesnake. We stared at each other for a moment. The snake began to rattle, and I turned and ran as hard as I could for Jim and

Ursula. I crawled under the wagon and lay there until they were ready to leave.

Jim was happier than I had ever seen him. He went on trips for Mr. Veramendi, who was now the vice-governor. He met some important people on his trips. Soon Jim owned a lot of land. His friends were able to get some land also, but no one had as much land as Jim. People liked him, and even the government officials he met wanted to be his friend.

One fine April day, Jim and Ursula were married. The wedding was a big event in San Antonio. After the wedding everyone attended a large party. Ursula was beautiful in her wedding gown, and Jim looked like a gentleman in his new clothes. They made a fine-looking couple. The party lasted all night. There was a band for people who wanted to dance, and there was a lot of good food. I visited nearly every table and was so full I had to lie down and take a nap.

The next day Jim and Ursula left for their honeymoon. I couldn't go. I had to stay with Mr. Veramendi. He was nice, but his little dog, Chico, drove me crazy with his yelping and snapping at my heels. I would turn and growl at him and he would run and hide, but soon he was back, yelping and snapping again. I was sure glad when Jim and Ursula came back. They acted like they were glad to see me too.

Jim settled down and began to look after his land. But I could tell that he was getting restless. Jim was not the kind of man who could be still for long. No matter how happy he was with Ursula, he needed to be out doing something, going somewhere new, searching for something different. His brother Rezin had come for the wedding, and he was still in San Antonio. Jim spent some time with him. They discussed plans to ride out on the plains to find new lands, but I could tell Jim really wanted to try to find the lost mines. According to the stories, the wealth of these mines would make Jim and Mr. Veramendi the richest men in the territory.

One day Mr. Veramendi sent for Jim. I went with him. A servant took us into Mr. Veramendi's office. Mr. Veramendi was sitting behind a desk looking at a map. He smiled and stood up as we entered.

"Welcome, Jim." He shook Jim's hand. "It's good to see you. I'm sorry I've been so busy that I haven't visited you. How is Ursula doing?"

"She's fine, sir. I'm a lucky man."

"Sit down, Jim. I think it's time we searched for the mines of San Saba."

Jim looked up. "The mines? Yes. I'm ready to find them."

Mr. Veramendi pointed to his map.

"Look here, Jim. I talked to a merchant who just came from that area. He said there are not many people there now. The Comanches have scared them away. Now is the time to look. There will not be people following you to find the mine. The merchant said that the mine is supposed to be in this area."

Jim looked at the map. He stared at the place where Mr. Veramendi was pointing.

"If the mine is in that area, it shouldn't be hard to find."

Mr. Veramendi shook his head.

"Don't be so sure, Jim. If it were that easy to find, someone would have found it long ago. You'll have to search the area carefully. I think it'll take you some time to completely search this place."

Jim smiled. "Well, Mr. Veramendi, I have nothing but time."

Mr. Veramendi shook his head.

"You'll have to be very careful, Jim. The merchant told me that the Comanches were in the area. They attacked his group and he was lucky to escape."

"I'll take enough men to fight off the Comanches. When do you want us to leave?"

Mr. Veramendi stood up.

"The day after tomorrow. I've already ordered the supplies you'll need; they should be ready for you. You must tell no one, not even Ursula, what you are searching for. If people hear about this, they'll follow you."

"I'll need to tell the men where we're going. I can't ask them to ride into Comanche territory and not know what they're doing."

Mr. Veramendi walked over to Jim.

"Wait until you're on the road for a day. Then anyone who wants to come back can. By the time they get here, you'll be too far for anyone to catch you. How many men will you take?"

Jim thought for a minute.

"I'll take ten, including my brother. That should be a large enough group to handle any Indians we might see."

Mr. Veramendi shook Jim's hand.

"All right. Your supplies will be waiting for you at the old mission just outside of town. The one they call the

Alamo. Good luck, Jim."

"Thank you, Mr. Veramendi. I think I'll need some luck."

As we walked down the street to Jim's house, he was silent. I could tell he was planning the trip to San Saba. Finally he looked at me and patted my head.

"When we find that mine, Gator, I'm going to get you a fancy collar. What do you think of that?"

I wagged my tail and licked his hand. I wished he would get me a nice bone instead.

Chapter Ten

THE SUN HAD SET, AND THE ONLY LIGHT came from our campfire. We had been traveling all day and the men were tired. The smell of roasting meat filled my nostrils as I lay next to Jim. A chill was in the air and the fire felt good. The men sat or lay around the fire. There was not much talking. Rezin and Turner checked on the horses and then walked back into our little circle. Rezin sat next to Jim while Turner carved some meat from the roasting buffalo.

"Are you going to tell us where we're going now?" Rezin asked Jim.

Jim stretched and looked around the circle.

"I guess now is a good time. We're headed to the area around the old San Saba Mission ruins."

Turner chewed his bite, then asked, "Why are we going there? There's nothing there but snakes and Indians."

Jim looked into the fire.

"There might be something else. Mr. Veramendi told me there's a story about a lost mine around there somewhere. He said that mine has more gold or silver than we could ever spend. That's what we're looking for."

The men were listening with interest. They would like to find the mine and get all that gold or silver. Turner reached for another slice of meat.

"Why are we being so sneaky? Why didn't you tell us this before?"

"Mr. Veramendi didn't want others to know. He was afraid they'd follow us. They'd certainly be in our way."

Rezin stood up and brushed the dirt from his pants.

"Well, I'm ready to go find this mine. What time do we start tomorrow?"

"It's not that easy," Jim said. "It seems there are some Comanche war parties in that area. We want to try and avoid them. Now, if any of you want to go back to San Antonio in the morning, you are free to do so."

The men laughed.

"Jim," Turner said. "You just told us there was a mine out there that was going to make us all rich. Now you want to know if we want to leave? I don't know about the others, but I'm with you."

The other men nodded their agreement.

"Good." Jim smiled. "Remember. There are Comanche war parties out there. Don't go wandering off. Make sure somebody knows where you are all the time. Keep your eyes open. We cannot afford to be caught by surprise.

Now let's get to sleep. We have a long way to go tomorrow."

The men rolled up in their blankets and were soon asleep. I watched the meat slowly cooking on the fire. The smell of the meat was making me awfully hungry. I walked over and tried to figure out how I could get that meat. Suddenly I had an idea. I jumped over the fire and grabbed the meat in my mouth. I landed on the other side of the fire and the meat fell to the ground. My tail was scorched, but otherwise I was not hurt. I lay next to the meat and waited for it to cool down. Soon I was eating the meat. It tasted as good as it smelled. Soon my stomach was full. I walked over next to Jim, lay down and went to sleep.

The next morning we were up early. We were riding toward San Saba before the sun had risen. The cool morning air felt good as we made our way across the prairie. The miles melted away and we were soon pausing on top of a small hill. Jim and the others looked around carefully, but there was no sign of any Indians. We rode on because Jim wanted to find a river to camp by that night. Late in the afternoon we found a small stream and made camp. The men's spirits were high as they settled down to sleep.

A few days later, Jim thought we were getting close to San Saba. He called Turner and Rezin up beside him.

"I think we'll leave the others in the oak grove. I want you to come with me while I check out the area."

Soon we were riding across the prairie looking for signs of the lost mine. The men were talking and I was trotting ahead of them, sniffing the air and looking for a rabbit to chase. Suddenly I smelled something. I noticed that the horses were acting like they smelled it too. The men looked around, but there was nothing on the prairie except us. We rode on. The smell was becoming stronger. It smelled like horses and paint and sweat. The horses were looking around and trying to turn back. I had an uneasy feeling as we came to the top of a small hill. We stopped and looked down into the small valley.

As we looked into the valley I saw what I had been smelling. There on the valley floor was a large band of Comanche Indians riding their painted, sweating horses. They had been riding hard, tracking us. I looked up at Jim and the others. They were staring down at the Indians. The Indians did not seem to see us. I thought that if we were very quiet, we might be able to get off the hill and get back to the rest of our party. Jim and the others quietly turned their horses around and started down the hill.

I trotted along beside Jim. I thought we had gotten away from the war party when one of the Indians looked up on the hill and saw us. He gave a loud war cry, and I turned to see the Indians riding as fast as they could toward us. I turned and saw Jim and the other two men riding toward the oak grove. I chased after them as fast as I could run. Behind me I could hear the Indian war cries. An arrow stuck in the ground next to me. I ran faster. I looked past Jim. The oak grove looked very far away, and the Indians sounded really close.

Chapter Eleven

"GRAMPA. DID THE INDIANS GET YOU?" Princess snuggled next to the old dog.

"'Course not." Butch growled at her. "He wouldn't be here telling the story if they had."

The old dog put a paw on Princess' head.

"I'll tell you what happened."

The pups lay next to the old dog as he continued his tale…

"I tell you I never ran so fast in my life. I could hear the Indians yelling, and I could feel the ground shaking from the pounding of their horses' hooves. Jim and his friends were riding as fast as they could toward the oak grove. It seemed like the trees were moving away from us.

Suddenly I saw some smoke coming from the trees. Then I heard the sound of the rifles being fired and soon bullets were whizzing over my head, heading toward the Comanches. The Indians stopped their horses and rode back out of range of the rifles. I saw Jim and the others disappear into the trees. Soon I was in the trees, and I ran under a bush and lay there trying to catch my breath. The horses were placed further into the grove, and then Jim joined the rest of the group as they watched the Indians sitting on their horses looking at us. One of the Indians rode his large black horse a few steps closer to us. He rode in several tiny circles, then stopped as if he was waiting for us to answer him.

"What's he doing?" Jim asked.

"He wants to talk to us," one of the men said.

"Do you speak their language, Juan?" Jim asked.

Juan Abamillo shook his head. "No. I know the sign language, and some of them speak Spanish."

Jim stood up. "Come with me, Juan. I guess we need to find out what he wants."

Jim and Juan rode out onto the prairie. They stopped before they got too far from the oak grove. The Comanche rode to them. I had followed Jim and I stood behind his horse. I was ready to run back to the trees if anything went wrong. The Indian made a sign of peace. Juan answered him. The Indian began to speak, but Juan shook his head, indicating he did not understand. The Indian began speaking in Spanish. Juan listened, then told Jim what had been said.

"He says he's the chief of this band. They've been

down in Mexico looking for horses and cattle. They were on their way home when they saw us. Some of his men are watching the livestock. The rest are here. He says this is his land. He wants to know what we're doing here."

Jim looked at the Indian chief. He wore a long feathered headdress, and his face was streaked with red and yellow paint. I thought he was the scariest-looking thing I had ever seen.

"Tell him we come as friends. We'll only be here a few days. Then we'll leave. Tell him we mean no harm to him or his tribe."

Juan spoke to the chief. He listened as the Indian answered him. When the chief had finished speaking, Juan turned to Jim.

"He says we must give him our horses and guns. He's hungry also, and would like to have your dog."

I backed up when I heard Juan say that. I had heard that Indians liked to eat dog meat, but I was not going to be his dinner.

Jim shook his head. "Tell him we won't give him our horses and guns, and he cannot have my dog. There's plenty of game around here if he's hungry."

I felt better when Jim said that. I kept my eye on the Indian. He listened carefully as Juan told him what Jim had said. The Indian was angry and spoke loudly to Juan. Juan looked at Jim.

"He says if you won't give him your horses and guns, then he'll take them. He'll also take your dog, although he thinks it's too skinny to make a good meal."

Jim pulled his knife from its scabbard. He held the big blade toward the chief.

"Tell him that this is waiting for him. Before he can have my rifle, horse or dog, he has to get past my knife."

Juan told the chief what Jim had said. The Indian angrily turned his horse around and rode back to where his braves had been watching. Jim and Juan quickly rode back to the trees and got off their horses. The men gathered around Jim.

"What did he want, Jim?" Rezin asked.

"Not much. Just our rifles and horses. And Gator. I don't think he liked it when I told him no."

"What are they going to do?" Turner asked.

Just then the chief gave a loud war cry. The men looked up in time to see the chief point his lance toward the oak grove and kick his black pony forward in a fast run. The other Indians followed him, yelling loudly.

Jim looked at the onrushing Indian warriors.

"I think he's going to try and take what he wants," he said.

Chapter Twelve

THE WAR CRIES OF THE INDIANS filled the air. I looked out from under my bush and saw them charging directly at us. I heard Jim talking to the men as I ducked back under the bush.

"Don't all fire at once. You five. Shoot first. While they're reloading, the other five shoot. After you shoot, move to a new position while you reload. They can't see us in these trees, so they'll shoot at the gun flash. Let them get closer. Make your shots count. They have a lot more men than we do. If they get to us, we're done for."

The Indians kept coming. Suddenly five rifles fired at the charging warriors. The smoke from the rifles filled the oak grove and made it hard to see. I could hear the pounding of the Indian horses' hooves. Five more rifles fired. When the smoke cleared, I looked out from under the bush. The Indians had ridden back out of range of the rifles. Arrows were sticking out of some trees. I saw an arrow lying on the ground next to me. The men were quickly reloading their rifles.

"Do you think they'll charge again, Jim?" Turner asked.

Jim looked out at the Indians. The chief who had spoken to Jim was riding up and down in front of the other Indians. We could hear him talking to the warriors.

"I think they'll come again. I think that chief is trying to talk them into it."

The chief turned his black horse toward us. He pointed his spear and yelled. His horse charged forward and the other Indians followed. Their war cries hurt my ears, and I crawled back under the bush. For several hours the oak grove was filled with smoke as the men fired at the Comanches, who charged us again and again. Late in the afternoon the Indians pulled back and we could see them talking. The tired Texans sat or lay on the ground as they waited for another attack.

Jim walked among the men. He asked each one how they were and how much ammunition they had left. Jim looked worried when he had finished checking the men. He walked to the center of a clearing and looked at the distant Indians. He turned back to the men who were watching him.

"We're nearly out of powder and ammunition. If they charge us again, you must be sure and make every shot count. It's getting late. If we can hold out until dark, we might have a chance to get away."

Turner wiped the black powder from his face.

"I tell you, Jim. I'd trade my part of that lost mine right now for a nice cold drink of water."

"You have as much chance of finding that mine right now as you do of getting a drink," Rezin said. "Where are we going to go when it gets dark, Jim?"

Jim looked at the sun as it began to set in the west.

"We're going back to San Antonio. If you get lost, just head east until you hit the San Antonio road. There are too many Comanches around here to keep looking for that mine."

A yell from the Indians sent the men running to find cover. The Indians charged toward the oak grove once again, but just before they came into range of the rifles, they turned their horses and rode toward the west. We all watched as the Indians disappeared into the distance.

"Do you think it's a trick, Jim?" Turner asked.

"I don't know," Jim said. "We're going to wait until it's dark, then we're headed back to San Antonio. Until then, be alert. The Indians might come back."

We stayed in the oak grove long after the sun had set. There were clouds in the sky that covered the moon and the stars. This would be good for us as we made our escape. Finally Jim stood up.

"Let's go," he whispered. "Just walk your horses. Pay attention. We don't know where those Indians might be."

We headed back across the prairie toward San Antonio. I trotted ahead of the horses. I sniffed the air, but I did not smell anything, no war paint or strange horses. Jim rode behind the others. He constantly checked to see if the Indians were trailing us. After we had been traveling for several hours, he rode to the head of the column.

"I think we're going to be all right," he said. "I think the Indians have had enough."

You could hear the men as they let their breath out.

"I tell you, Jim," Rezin said. "That's about as scared as I've ever been. We've been in some tight spots before, but never one as bad as this."

I could see Jim smile.

"I think you're right. That was a real tough spot. I hate to tell Mr. Veramendi that we didn't find the mines, but at least we all have our scalps."

A couple of days later we rode into San Antonio. The people on the streets looked at us as we headed toward our house. You could tell they were wondering where we had been and what we had been doing. A couple of dogs barked at me from the doorway of a house, but I didn't care. It was good to be home.

Chapter Thirteen

FOR SEVERAL MONTHS AFTER THE SEARCH for the lost mines, Jim stayed home and looked after his land. He and Ursula were happy and Jim talked about never leaving San Antonio again. One day Mr. Veramendi called Jim to his office. I went with Jim to see the vice-governor. Mr. Veramendi smiled as we walked into his office.

"Jim. Good to see you. Sit down. Would you like something to drink?"

"No, thank you," Jim said as he sat down. "What did you want to see me about, Governor?"

Mr. Veramendi looked at the papers on his desk for several minutes. Finally he looked up at Jim.

"I'm afraid that things aren't going well. President

Santa Anna thinks that all the new settlers are a danger to Mexico. He wants to stop any further settlements. He even wants to force the settlers who are here to leave. I'm afraid that there'll be a war."

"Do you really think Santa Anna will fight the settlers?"

Mr. Veramendi nodded.

"Yes I do, Jim. I've met the man. He's very proud. He thinks the settlers want to take Texas away from Mexico. He thinks they want to join the United States. He thinks that this would be a great insult. I have heard he has sent a commander named Jose de las Piedras to Nacogdoches to take the weapons away from the settlers there. I'm afraid there will be a fight."

"If he tries to take their weapons, there will be a fight," Jim said. "What do you want me to do?"

"Take some men to Nacogdoches. See what's going on and do what you can to see that he doesn't harm the settlers."

Jim stood up. "I better find some men."

"I have already found you some. They'll be in the plaza in the morning."

Mr. Veramendi looked troubled.

"What else is wrong, Governor?" Jim asked.

"An epidemic of cholera is moving through the country. I'm afraid it will come here. It's a deadly disease. I'm worried about our families."

"I agree. You can't stay here. I know, take everyone to Monclova. It's healthier there. I think you'll be all right there. After I check on Nacogdoches, I'll come there to be with you."

Mr. Veramendi smiled.

"That's a good idea. I'll leave in a couple of days. Tell Ursula she'll come with us."

Jim turned toward the door.

"I'll see you in a couple of weeks. Take good care of Ursula."

We walked back home. Ursula was sitting in the front room reading a book. She smiled as we walked in.

"What did my father want?" she asked.

Jim sat beside her. "I have to go to Nacogdoches on a mission for him. I should be back in a couple of weeks. He wants you to go to Monclova with him and your mother. I'll come there when I get back."

"Why does he want to go to Monclova? There's a lot to do here. I have a lot of work to do on our home. I can't go to Monclova for a few weeks. I'll tell him I'm staying here."

Jim took Ursula's hand.

"Ursula, just go with him. It would upset him if he thought you didn't want to go with him. There's plenty of time to work on the house."

Ursula looked at Jim and smiled.

"Oh, all right. I guess it will be fun to get out of town for a while. Don't be gone too long. I'll miss you."

"I'll miss you too. Now I have to get ready to leave. I'm supposed to leave in the morning."

Early the next morning I trotted beside Jim's horse as we rode to the plaza. A group of men waited for us. Jim stopped in front of the men.

"Everybody ready?"

"We're ready," one of the men said.

"Well then, let's head for Nacogdoches."

It took us several days to make the journey to Nacogdoches. As we came in sight of the city, a rider came toward us. The men readied their rifles as the rider came nearer. When he stopped his horse in front of Jim, we saw he was a settler.

"Hello. Would you happen to be Jim Bowie?"

"I am."

The man smiled and stuck out his hand. "I'm sure glad to see you. My name's Jenkins. I have a house right outside of town. We heard you were coming."

"Are there Mexican soldiers in the area?"

"Yes. They're in the town. They want us to give up our weapons, but we're not going to."

Jim looked toward the town.

"Would you show us where the best place to get these soldiers out of your town would be?"

The man turned his horse. "Follow me."

Jim turned to the men behind him. "Come on, boys. We have to escort some soldiers out of town."

Chapter Fourteen

As we approached the town, a sentry saw us and gave the alarm. We could see the townspeople running for their homes and the Mexican soldiers forming a line. Soon a bugle call could be heard.

Jim pointed toward the town.

"Come on, boys," Jim called. He pointed toward the soldiers. "Let's go get them."

The men cheered and ran toward the soldiers. Soon rifle balls filled the air. I heard them as they whizzed by my ears. I dropped back behind the men. I saw Jim out in front. He was yelling and pointing his knife at the soldiers.

Soon black clouds of powder smoke filled the air and I could no longer see what was happening. I saw an open doorway and rushed inside. It was dark inside the house. As my eyes grew used to the darkness, I saw an enemy soldier pointing his rifle out of the window. I growled and bared my teeth at the man. He turned and pointed his gun at me. I barked and the man's eyes grew wide. He dropped his rifle and turned and ran out of the back door. I was feeling proud of myself. I had scared off an enemy soldier. I turned to walk out of the door and I saw Jim standing there with his big knife in his hand. It was Jim who had scared the soldier, not me. I ducked my head and started to walk past Jim when he reached down and patted my head.

"Good boy. You showed me where that soldier was." He patted me again.

I felt good again. I had helped. The shooting had stopped. We walked down the street. One of Jim's men came running up to us.

"Jim, the enemy's run away."

"Where have they gone?" Jim asked.

The man pointed down the road.

"They went down that road. They were running as fast as they could. What do we do now?"

Jim looked where the man had pointed.

"We're going to follow them. I want to make sure they don't come back."

Soon we were riding after the enemy. In a short period of time we could see the dust raised by their horses as they raced down the road. Before long we found the enemy resting by a stream. They were giving their horses a drink. We stopped in a small group of trees and watched them.

"They don't know we're here," Jim said. "Get ready. When I tell you, fire your rifles then charge them. They'll be surprised. Don't give them time to shoot back."

The men waited for Jim to tell them to shoot. When he gave the signal, the men fired their rifles. The enemy looked at the trees. They could see the smoke from our rifles. Then they saw the men as they charged from the trees. The men were yelling and shooting as fast as they could. The enemy took one look at the screaming Texans and ran away. We chased them for a while, and then Jim raised his hand to stop the attack.

"That's far enough. Let them go. I don't think they'll come back."

The men stopped and watched the enemy run away. We rode back to the stream and drank the cool water. Jim sat with his back against a tree. I lay beside him with my head in his lap. Now that the fighting was over, we were tired. One of the men walked over and sat beside Jim.

"What are we going to do now?"

Jim looked at the men lying under the trees.

"We'll rest here until tomorrow and then head back to San Antonio. I'm ready to see Ursula again. They should be back from Monclova by now."

That night I looked at the stars while Jim and the others slept. The moon was full and its light lit up the prairie. I was ready to get back home too. I missed Ursula. She was always nice to me. I could hardly wait for the morning to come. Finally the sun peeked above the horizon. The camp began to stir as the men woke up. I sat next to Jim, gnawing on a bone as he drank some coffee. The men were cooking their breakfast and getting ready to leave.

Suddenly I heard the sound of horses' hooves. The rider was coming fast. Soon he was in view. Jim and the others watched him as he came closer.

"Can you tell who it is?" one of the men asked.

Jim shook his head.

"Not yet. He sure is in a hurry though."

Finally the rider came close enough to recognize.

"That's Turner. I've never seen him ride like that," one of the men said.

Soon Turner dragged his horse to a stop in front of the campfire. He got down off his horse and walked over to Jim.

Jim stuck out his hand. "Good to see you, Turner. Looks like you've been riding hard. Have a seat and pour yourself some coffee."

Turner looked at Jim.

"Thanks, Jim, but I'm afraid I have some bad news."

"What is it, Turner?" Jim asked. "Is there another army coming?"

Turner shook his head. "No." Turner looked down at the ground. "Jim, the cholera went through Monclova. Ursula, Mr. Veramendi, the whole family is dead."

I looked up at Jim. His face was white. He did not say anything for a while. Finally he looked up. I saw a tear roll down his cheek.

"Come on, men. We have to get home," he said softly.

Chapter
Fifteen

"IT MAKES ME SAD TO HEAR that Ursula died," Princess said.

The old dog put his paw on her head.

"It made Jim sad too. For months he just wandered around their house. I think he expected Ursula to come out of one of the rooms. Jim was never the same after that."

Butch rolled over and watched a cloud pass by.

"Tell us about some more Indian fights."

The old dog yawned. He was thinking about the old days…

"There were no more Indian fights. The days dragged

into months and the months dragged into years. Jim tried to keep busy with his land, but he was not a good businessman. He lost a lot of his land. Jim tried to find the lost mines one more time, but had no luck. More people came into Texas, and the relationship with Mexico became worse and worse. Stephen Austin tried to calm things down, but young hotheads like William Travis kept things stirred up.

Jim became very interested in what was going on. He joined the men who wanted to separate from Mexico. As time went on everyone knew that there would be a war. Stephen Austin went to Mexico to try and work things out, but he was thrown in jail. After a year he came home, and now even Austin believed that war was coming.

Austin raised an army of volunteers and marched toward San Antonio. The army camped on Cibolo Creek, and Jim joined them with some of his friends. Austin was glad to see Jim. He walked up to us as we rode into the camp.

"Good to see you, Jim. We can use men like you."

"Hello, Mr. Austin. We heard you were headed to San Antonio so we thought we would join up and see what we can find."

Austin led Jim into his tent. I followed them and curled up in a corner.

"Jim, I think there will be a fight when we get to San Antonio. You have lived there for awhile, tell me about the town."

"Well, let's see. A lot of the people there don't like Santa Anna. But they're not sure your army can win. So they're going to try and stay out of the fight. Juan Seguin will fight with us. He has a few men. I think most of the people are going to wait and see what happens. There's an old mission there called the Alamo. The Mexican army has been working on it in case they need a fort. It's not a fort, though, it's a mission and wasn't built to be a fort."

Austin listened carefully to Jim.

"I want you to take some men and scout out the town. Find out what's happening and let me know."

Jim shook his head. "I have no authority over these men."

Austin smiled. "As commander of this army, I'm placing you on my staff with the rank of colonel. Now you can lead the men."

Jim smiled. "Colonel. That sounds mighty important. When do you want me to leave?"

"In the morning. I want you to check out the Mission Concepcion near San Antonio. There's a man here I want you to take with you. He is Captain James Fannin. He might be of some help. He went to West Point for a year."

Jim stood up.

"All right, sir. I'll be glad to take Captain Fannin. I'll tell the men to be ready to leave the first thing in the morning."

Early the next morning, Jim and ninety other men rode out of the camp. We headed toward San Antonio. Fall was in the air, but the day warmed up as the sun rose higher in the sky. I felt good as I trotted alongside Jim's horse. Every now and then a rabbit would jump up from the high grass. I would chase him, but I never caught a single rabbit. As we got closer to San Antonio, I could hear a bell ringing in the distance. It was a bell at one of the missions. Jim stopped his horse and listened to the bell. Captain Fannin rode up beside Jim.

"Why is the bell ringing, Colonel? Do you think they know we're coming?"

Jim shook his head.

"No. It's getting to be time for the evening services. We should be getting close to Mission Concepcion. We'll wait here until dark. Then we'll check out the area."

When the sun set, we rode to the old mission. There was no one around. Jim went into the mission. It was empty, but there were signs that someone had been there not long before. Jim walked back outside and spoke to the waiting men.

"It looks like the people have left. They probably saw us coming and ran to town. That means that the Mexican army will know we're here. I want the guards to keep a close watch tonight. I don't want to wake up tomorrow and see a Mexican soldier looking down at me."

Guards were posted and soon those not on guard duty were asleep. We did not light any fires because Jim did not want to show the enemy where we were. The men ate cold bread and cheese. I tried to find some meat scraps or a bone, but I couldn't find any and my stomach was growling as I lay down next to Jim. I finally went to sleep. I woke up early in the morning. A fog covered the area making it hard to see. I thought I heard the sound of someone walking. I listened but could not tell what it was. Suddenly one of the sentries shouted.

"Colonel Bowie. The enemy's coming. A lot of them!"

Chapter Sixteen

As the enemy emerged from the fog, I hid under a table next to the old mission. I could hear them yelling as they charged us. Then the rifles began to fire and the shouts could no longer be heard. I saw Jim run by me. I heard him yell to the men to keep their aim low. The flashes from the rifles lit up the foggy morning. Suddenly there was a loud roar. The enemy was firing a cannon at us. I crouched as low as I could to the ground as a cannonball passed over my head. I heard the ball thud against the side of the mission.

"Stay down, men," Jim shouted.

The cannon fired again.

"There it is," one of the men yelled.

Jim called to two of the men to join him. He pointed to the spot from where the cannon had fired.

"Be ready. When they fire again, aim for the gunners. We need to stop that cannon from firing."

The men watched until the cannon fired again. They fired at the blast from the cannon. I heard the sound of feet running away in the fog. The cannon did not fire again. The rest of the men were firing at the charging enemy. Soon the enemy stopped their charge and looked for places to hide. I could hear their officers yelling for them to charge again, but the fire from the Texans kept the enemy lying down behind whatever cover they could find.

The battle lasted for several hours. Suddenly the enemy soldiers got to their feet and ran back into the fog, leaving their cannon behind. Jim and the others stayed behind their cover until they were sure that the enemy had left. Jim had the men hitch the cannon to some horses, and we pulled it back to where Stephen Austin and the rest of the army were waiting. Jim reported what had happened.

"That's good, Jim," Austin said. "I've found out that Santa Anna's brother- in-law, General Cos, is in San Antonio with his army."

"What are your plans?" Jim asked.

"I'm going to attack General Cos and force him and his army out of Texas. I hear they're in an old mission called the Alamo. I don't think it can stand up to a strong attack."

"I'm familiar with the Alamo," Jim said. "It's a ruin. Unless they've done a lot of repairs, it's not a good place to try and fight from."

"I agree," Austin said. "We're going to march to San Antonio tomorrow. Let your men rest. They have been fighting hard and they're probably tired."

Jim nodded. "They're tired. But, we'll be ready tomorrow."

I walked beside Jim as we found a spot under a large tree. Jim sat down and leaned against the tree while I lay beside him and put my head in his lap. Soon we were both asleep. I was dreaming of eating a large, juicy steak when I heard someone shouting Jim's name. I looked up and saw Juan Seguin running toward us.

"Wake up, Jim," Juan shouted.

Jim stood up and rubbed his eyes. "What's the matter, Juan?"

Juan came to a stop in front of Jim. "Austin wants to see you right away."

Jim looked around. "It's not morning yet, Juan. He said to get some rest because we were leaving in the morning."

"Yes, I know. But word has just come from town that a pack train is heading toward San Antonio."

"So what?" Jim said as he sat back down. "The pack train won't reach San Antonio until tomorrow."

Juan grabbed Jim's hand and pulled him to his feet. "Jim, this is not an ordinary pack train."

Jim brushed off his pants. "Well what makes this one so special?"

"Someone from San Antonio came to see Austin. They told him that this pack train was carrying a large shipment of gold for the enemy army."

Jim was wide-awake now. "Gold? What does Austin want me to do?"

"He wants you to take your men and go get the gold. We need it for our own army."

Jim started walking toward Austin's tent. He turned back to me.

"Come on, Gator. If that train is carrying gold, I'll be able to buy you all the steak you can eat."

I ran ahead of Jim. If getting that gold meant I was going to eat steak, I was going to see that we found that pack train before it reached San Antonio.

Chapter Seventeen

"Did you find the gold, Grampa?" Princess asked.

"I would rather have all the steak," Butch said.

The old dog shook his head.

"If you two will hush for a minute, I'll tell you…"

"We rode through the countryside as fast as we could, trying to reach the enemy caravan before it arrived in San Antonio. I raced alongside Jim's horse. The thought of all that steak made me run faster. One of the scouts that Jim had sent ahead of us came riding back as fast as he could. Jim stopped the men and waited for the scout. The scout's horse was breathing hard as he came to a stop in front of Jim.

"The caravan is about a mile away," he said, pointing in the direction he had come from.

"How many men are there?" Jim asked.

The scout took off his hat and scratched his head.

"I would say about one hundred fifty to two hundred. They don't seem to be in any hurry to move along."

Jim nodded.

"Good. That means they're not worried about being attacked."

Jim looked around the prairie. "Let's head in that direction. We can get ahead of them and cut them off."

We rode hard for a couple of miles. We came to a grove of trees next to a small stream. Jim signaled the men to stop.

"We'll wait here. Let your horses rest. Keep in the trees so the enemy can't see you. When they get in front of that little hill, we'll attack."

The men waited in the trees and watched for the enemy to appear. Suddenly the lead riders came over the rise. We waited until the whole column was at the bottom of the little hill. They were riding in a long line. There were no scouts searching the area, and I could hear the soldiers talking as they rode slowly along. Jim gave the signal, and the men fired at the surprised enemy soldiers. They tried to form a line to fight us, but we charged at them and they began to run.

I saw a soldier trying to lead a mule away. I saw the bags hanging on the sides of the mule and I thought about the gold in the sacks and how many steaks that would buy. I ran at the soldier and bit him in the seat of his pants. He yelled and swung his rifle at me. The rifle hit me in the side, and I rolled in the tall grass. I got to my feet and started to attack the soldier again. He raised his rifle to shoot at me. I jumped to the side as the rifle fired. The bullet hit the ground next to me. I barked and ran toward the soldier. He turned and ran away, leaving the mule with his packs.

The firing had stopped, and I saw the Texans rounding up the mules. Soon all of the mules were standing in a line. Jim walked up to the first mule and pulled out his knife.

"Let's see how much gold this mule can carry," he said.

He sliced the sack open. The men watched with great interest. My stomach growled as I thought of all the juicy steaks the gold would buy. Jim reached his hand into the sack and pulled out a handful of… grass. He held it up for the men to see.

"Looks like there's no gold here," he said.

One of the men called out. "Check some more. They might have packed grass around the gold to keep it from clanking."

Jim reached his hand into the sack again. I saw him feeling around in the sack. He pulled his hand out again, and once again he had a handful of grass.

The men murmured with disappointment. Finally one of them yelled to Jim.

"This mule probably carries the grass to feed the other mules. Check some of the others."

Jim walked to the next mule. This mule also carried only grass. My stomach growled with hunger as I watched Jim walk down the line of mules and check their loads.

Each time he pulled out several handfuls of grass. At last he reached the end of the line. None of the mules carried any gold. The men walked away. They were all disappointed. The scout who had found the caravan walked up to Jim.

"What do you think happened to the gold, Jim?"

Jim looked at the open sacks hanging from the mules with grass showing through the openings.

"I think we got the wrong information. This group was gathering grass to feed the enemy's horses in San Antonio. I don't know where the story about the gold came from."

The scout laughed. "Well, I guess everybody back with the army will have a good laugh about the grass fight."

"I guess they will," Jim agreed. He looked down at me. "Come on, Gator. Let's go home."

I watched Jim walk over to his horse. I was really hungry and now there would be no steak. I looked up at the line of mules standing there with their sacks full of grass. Maybe I would just eat the mules. But with my stomach growling, I ran over and followed Jim home.

Chapter Eighteen

EVENTS MOVED RAPIDLY DURING THE NEXT couple of months. Jim left the army and went to Goliad. While he was there the Texans attacked General Cos, who had taken refuge in the old mission called the Alamo, and drove him from Texas. We heard about the battle while we were in Goliad. Jim had begun to cough a lot. He said it was just a cold, but it sounded much worse. The doctors at Goliad gave him some medicine, but it did not seem to help.

One day as Jim and I sat in the small room we shared, trying to keep warm, a messenger brought a letter to Jim. I watched him read it as I lay next to the fire. When he had finished reading the letter, he put it on the table and looked at me.

"Well, Gator. It seems that General Sam Houston wants me to see about leading a force against Matamoros. It seems several people think we should take the fight into Mexico instead of having them come here. What do you think?"

I yawned and stretched and lay back down by the fire with my head resting on my paws.

"That's what I think, too." Jim laughed and scratched my head. "I don't think we have enough men for that kind of war. Anyway, the word is that Santa Anna is heading this way with a large army. He's mad about our army kicking General Cos out of San Antonio. I think before long we'll have all the fighting we want, right here."

Jim started coughing. He lay on his bed and pulled some covers over him. I lay by the fire and watched his body shake from the coughing. I did not know what was wrong with Jim, but I had a bad feeling it was very serious.

Several weeks later, Jim came into our room. I looked up as he sat at the table and read another letter from General Houston.

"It seems that General Houston is coming here. He has another mission for me. He'll tell me what it is when he gets here. The government could not agree on a leader for the Matamoros expedition, so now he has a new plan. He should be here soon. I can't wait to hear his latest idea."

One day there was a knock on our door. Jim opened the door and a tall man was standing there. He wore a great coat to protect himself from the cold. Jim smiled and put out his hand when he recognized the man.

"General Houston. Good to see you. Come in and have a seat."

Houston walked into the room and sat down at the table. Jim sat across from him. "What can I do for you, General?"

Houston took off his coat and leaned back in his chair. "Jim, you know the rumors are that Santa Anna is on his way to Texas with a large army. In fact, the story is he's headed to San Antonio. He's mad about General Cos being run out of San Antonio, and he wants revenge."

Jim nodded.

"I've heard those stories."

Houston continued. "As you know, we have a small army there right now. Colonel Neill is in command. From all the reports I receive, the army is in bad shape. Little food or medicine. Their clothes are all rags. About the only thing they have plenty of is cannon."

Jim coughed. "I've heard they need a lot of things at San Antonio."

"You're one of the few men I can count on. I'm leaving to make a treaty with the Indians so they won't attack us while we fight Santa Anna. I have a very important job for you."

"What do you want me to do, General?"

"Jim, I want you to take some men to San Antonio, blow up the Alamo, and bring the cannon to Gonzales."

Jim sat up in his chair. "Blow up the Alamo? That's one of the key posts in keeping Santa Anna out of the colonies."

Houston shook his head. "We cannot fight Santa Anna from forts. We're not strong enough. The army is too small. We must fight him in the open where we can move, not be locked into a fort."

"Have you told Colonel Neill this?" Jim asked.

"You tell Colonel Neill I gave you orders to do this. He'll go along with my orders. I'll send some other men to help you. Do you know William Travis?"

Jim nodded.

"I'll send him with some more men."

Jim coughed then looked at Houston. "General, if we blow up the Alamo, we'll have nothing to stop Santa Anna."

"Jim, the Alamo won't stop Santa Anna. General Cos couldn't hold the Alamo and he had more men than we do. That place was not built as a fort. It was built as a mission. Can I count on you, Jim?"

Jim was silent for a moment as he thought about Houston's plan. Finally he said. "I'll go to San Antonio, General."

Houston stood up. "Good. I must be going. I have a long ride to the Indian village. I'll talk to you when I get back."

Houston started to leave, then turned back to Jim. "You better see a doctor about that cough."

Jim smiled and shook Houston's hand. "I have seen one, General. Don't worry. It's just a cold."

Chapter Nineteen

IT WAS GOOD TO SEE SAN ANTONIO AGAIN. I had spent many pleasant days in the town. The streets were crowded as we rode toward the Veramendi house. Thirty men had ridden with us. They were all Jim's friends and he knew he could count on them. As we rode down the street, someone called Jim's name. We turned to see Juan Seguin running toward us.

"Jim. It's good to see you. Welcome back to San Antonio."

Jim leaned down from his saddle and shook Juan's hand. "It's good to be back, Juan. This town has changed."

Juan nodded. "Yes. The battle of last December destroyed many houses. Many people have left. They're afraid that Santa Anna will return."

"What do you think, Juan?" Jim asked.

Juan removed his hat and ran his fingers through his hair. "I've heard from some of the vaqueros that live to the south that Santa Anna is already on the way here. He's bringing a large army. I think he'll be here before long."

Jim straightened up in the saddle. "I have a message for Colonel Neill from General Houston. Do you know where he is?"

Juan pointed toward the Alamo.

"I believe he's in the Alamo. He's trying to make it into a strong fort."

Jim looked toward the Alamo. "I'll go see him. But first, I want to stop by the Veramendi house. I'll talk to you later, Juan."

Juan stood in the street and watched us ride away. Soon we stopped in front of the Veramendi house. Jim dismounted while the rest of the men rode on to find a place to stay. We walked into the house. It was cool inside. A fire was burning in the fireplace, but it did not provide much warmth. Jim walked from room to room. I could tell he was thinking of the days when he had lived in this house with Ursula.

"Jim. It's so good to see you."

A woman ran from one of the rooms and hugged Jim.

"Juana. It's good to see you too. How have you been?"

"I've been fine, Jim. I married Dr. Alsbury. He's away on business right now. My sister Gertrudis is here. Do you remember her?"

"Of course I do." Jim walked over to the fire. "Are

you staying here?"

"Yes. There are plenty of rooms. You and your dog are welcome to stay here while you are in San Antonio."

Jim coughed, then warmed his hands by the fire.

"Thank you. I'm not sure how long I will be here. I have orders for Colonel Neill from General Houston. I must go to the Alamo. I've heard that's where Colonel Neill is."

Juana walked over and took Jim's hand. "Be back for supper. Gertrudis will want to see you."

"I'll be sure to be back."

Jim walked outside. He coughed and bent over to catch his breath. I was getting worried about him. I was beginning to think that the cough was caused by much more than a cold.

We rode into the Alamo. Several men were busy working on making the walls stronger. Some were placing cannons on the walls. Jim stopped beside a man who was sitting on a box.

"Excuse me," Jim said. "Can you tell me where Colonel Neill is?"

The man pointed toward a small room in one of the buildings. "His office is in there."

Jim rode over and stopped in front of the room. He got off his horse and knocked on the door.

"Come in," said a voice from inside.

We walked into the small room. As our eyes adjusted to the darkness, we saw a man sitting behind a small desk. He was staring out of the window.

"Colonel Neill. I'm Jim Bowie."

Colonel Neill sprang to his feet and walked over to

us. "I heard you were in town. I'm sure glad to see you. Have a seat."

Jim sat down. I sat next to him. Colonel Neill walked behind his desk and sat in his chair. "I guess you can see we're busy building this mission into a fort."

Jim nodded.

"Looks like you and your men have done a lot of work. The problem is I have orders from General Houston to blow up the Alamo and take the cannon to a safer place."

Neill stood up. "I don't believe it. After the fighting we did to take this place? After all the work to turn this mission into a fort? We can't just blow it up and leave."

Jim reached down and scratched my ears.

"General Houston is worried about our troops getting penned up in forts. He thinks we have a better chance of beating Santa Anna if we fight him in the open."

Neill walked over and looked out of the window.

"Jim, this place is the only thing standing between Santa Anna and the colonies. If we don't stop him here, or at least slow him down, he'll burn our towns and destroy our crops. People have come to Texas looking for a new life. The men here are willing to fight for that life. This is the place to make that fight."

"How many men do you have, Colonel?"

Neill shook his head. "Not many. Most of them went off on that crazy Matamoros expedition. But, I believe that reinforcements are being sent to us. We should have more men very soon. How many did you bring?"

"I brought thirty men. They're good men, but we need many more to hold this place."

"More will come, Jim. I think everyone understands the importance of San Antonio. You lived here. Don't you think it's worth fighting for?"

I watched Jim as he stared at the ceiling. I knew he was thinking about Ursula and Mr. Veramendi. He was thinking of all the happy times he had spent in San Antonio. Finally he stood up.

"Colonel Neill, you're right. We must stop Santa Anna, and the Alamo is the place to do it. I'm sure General Houston won't like it, but by the time he gets back from visiting with the Indians, we'll have whipped Santa Anna and sent him back home."

Chapter Twenty

THE NEXT COUPLE OF WEEKS WERE BUSY. William Travis arrived with thirty men. Travis and Jim had never gotten along too well. But then, not many men got along with Travis. Colonel Neill had to leave town to attend to some family business and left Travis in command of the troops. When the men found out they were mad. They wanted Jim to be their leader. An election was held and Jim was chosen to be the leader of the volunteer troops, while Travis continued to lead the regulars. Both men agreed to sign all letters and orders that were necessary.

The spirits of the men were raised one day when a company of men rode into town. I sat on the sidewalk and watched the men stop their horses in front of the building. A tall man wearing a coonskin hat walked up to me and scratched my ears.

"Hello, boy. How are you today?"

His voice was kind, and I licked his hand. Jim walked out of the building and walked over to us.

"Hello. My name's Jim Bowie. That's my dog, Gator."

The man stretched out his hand. "Glad to meet you. I've heard of you. My name's Davy Crockett."

Jim smiled. "Welcome, Davy. We are sure glad to see you."

Jim motioned for Davy to come into the office. Travis sat at a table writing a letter. Jim stood in front of him and pointed to Davy.

"Colonel Travis, this is the latest man to join us. Davy Crockett."

Travis jumped to his feet. He came around the desk and shook Davy's hand. "Very glad to meet you. We can sure use men like you."

The men sat down around the desk.

"Tell me what's going on here," Davy said.

Travis leaned back in his chair. "We're waiting for Santa Anna to come back here. We've heard that he's on his way with his army. But I don't think he'll come until the spring. It would be too hard to move a large army across the prairies in the winter. He'll wait for spring so his horses will have green grass to eat."

Davy saw Jim frowning. "You don't agree, Jim?"

Jim shook his head. "Juan Seguin's men report that Santa Anna is already getting close. This dead grass makes good food for the horses. I believe he'll be here soon."

Davy looked at both men. "I didn't see too many

men when I rode into town. How do you plan to stop Santa Anna's army?"

Travis stood up and walked to a window.

"We're fortifying that old mission across the river. The Alamo. We've sent requests for reinforcements to the government, and we expect General Houston to send us more men at any time."

Davy scratched his head. "I don't know if I like the idea of being penned up in a fort. I like to be able to move around."

Jim nodded. "I agree with you, Davy. But we'll hold Santa Anna here for a little while, then more men will come and we can send him back to Mexico."

Davy stood up. He stuck out his hand to Jim. Jim coughed and then took Davy's hand.

"That's a bad cough, Jim. You should have the doctor give you some medicine."

"I've been to the doctor. I think it's only a bad cold."

Davy shook Travis's hand. "I'd better find a place for my men to stay."

"We're glad to have you here, Davy," Travis said.

Davy waved as he walked out of the door.

"I told you more men would come," Travis said to Jim. "With men like Davy Crockett, we can hold the Alamo against Santa Anna as long as we need to."

Jim coughed and sat down in the chair. "He's a good man, but we need many more men to hold this place."

Travis sat down and began to write another letter.

"They will come, Jim. They will come."

A few more men did come during the next several weeks. Work on the Alamo continued. Jim was getting weaker every day, but he tried not to let anyone know how sick he was. Colonel Travis finally agreed to post sentries to watch for the approach of the enemy army. One morning I was sleeping at the foot of Jim's bed. I was dreaming of a nice, juicy bone. Suddenly a bell began to ring. Jim jumped from his bed. He coughed as he pulled on his clothes, then we ran outside. People were coming from their houses. Everyone looked at the bell tower, where the sentry was pulling the rope as hard as he could. Colonel Travis ran to the bottom of the tower and yelled up to the sentry.

"What's wrong?"

The sentry pointed towards the open prairie. "The enemy are in view," he yelled.

Chapter Twenty-one

THE STREETS OF SAN ANTONIO WERE FILLED with people running in all directions. Some were headed out of town; others were rushing toward the Alamo. Travis was trying to put some order into those headed toward the old mission, but most ignored him and rushed to get inside the walls. Jim found a wagon and drove to the Veramendi house. Juana and Gertrudis ran out of the house as Jim was getting down from the wagon.

"Jim, what's happening?" Juana asked.

"Santa Anna's army's here. We need to get inside the Alamo," Jim said as he walked into the house.

The women followed him inside.

"Get some of your things and climb in the wagon,"

Jim said.

"What should we take?" Gertrudis asked.

"Nothing big. Just some clothes and maybe something small you really value. Everything else we have to leave."

The women ran to get their things. Jim started coughing and sat in a chair. There was a chill in the air, but sweat rolled down Jim's face. I thought he looked worse than I had ever seen him. He looked at me and scratched my ears. I licked his hand. It felt warm. The women came back and Jim loaded their bags on the wagon. We drove toward the Alamo. I rode in the back of the wagon.

As we neared the old mission, I saw the first men of Santa Anna's army entering San Antonio. Inside the Alamo men climbed to the top of the walls to look at the enemy army, while the women and children tried to find a place to stay in the old chapel. I saw Susannah Dickinson carrying her baby into the chapel. Her husband, Almeron, was one of the men standing by a cannon, watching the enemy enter the town.

Jim sent the women into the chapel and then climbed onto the wall. I stood beside him. I could see through a crack in the wall. The enemy army was much larger than the small group of Texans. I saw a large red flag flying from a flagpole in the center of San Antonio.

One of the men shouted to Juan Sequin.

"What does that flag mean?"

Juan took off his hat and wiped his forehead. "It means they'll give us no mercy when the fighting starts."

The men stared silently at the flag flapping in the breeze. Travis walked over to Jim.

"Do you have any suggestions, Jim?"

Jim shook his head. He pointed toward a rider heading toward the Alamo. "I think we're about to find out what Santa Anna's thinking," he said.

Soon the enemy officer stopped his horse in front of the Alamo walls. He pulled out a sheet of paper and read a message from Santa Anna. The message said that the Texans should surrender. Santa Anna would then decide what he would do with the men. If they did not surrender, he would attack the Alamo without mercy.

Jim looked at Travis. "What do you say to that?"

Travis looked at Captain Dickinson. "Fire the cannon," Travis shouted.

Captain Dickinson put his torch to the powder, and the cannon roared. The men watched as the cannonball bounced down the main street of San Antonio. It finally came to rest against the wall of a small house. The enemy messenger turned and rode back toward the enemy army.

Travis turned to Jim. "What do you think of my answer?"

Jim looked at the enemy soldiers moving around in the town.

"I say you spoke very loudly and very clearly. And now we've got a fight on our hands."

Jim started coughing and leaned against the cannon for support.

"Jim." Travis walked over to him. "You should go and see Dr. Pollard."

Jim waved him away. "I've been to see him. There's nothing he can do. Excuse me, Colonel Travis, I need to see about my sisters-in-law."

I followed Jim down the ramp. We walked across the courtyard toward the chapel. Jim staggered as he walked. He stopped several times to catch his breath. He looked down at me and smiled.

"It sure is a long way across this courtyard. I don't remember it being so far."

He coughed again, then started walking toward the chapel. I heard the roar of an enemy cannon being fired. The cannonball whistled as it flew through the air. It landed in the courtyard and exploded, throwing dirt and metal all around. I ducked under a wagon when I heard the cannonball coming. When the smoke cleared away, I looked out from under the wagon. Jim lay on the ground. He was not moving.

Chapter
Twenty-two

"DID THE CANNONBALL HIT JIM?" Princess asked as tears filled her eyes.

The old dog licked her face as he went on with his story...

"I ran to Jim as fast as I could. The dust and smoke still filled the air. I sniffed him and licked his face. There was no blood, but Jim's face was covered with sweat. Colonel Travis, Davy Crockett, and several other men rushed over to us. They pushed me aside as they kneeled by Jim.

"Where's Dr. Pollard?" Travis called.

A man pushed his way through the crowd. "Here I

am."

He felt Jim's head then checked his body for wounds. "He wasn't hit by the cannonball," he said.

"What's wrong with him?" Davy Crockett asked.

Dr. Pollard felt Jim's head again. "He's very sick. I'm not sure what it is, but it's very serious." He looked at the crowd. "Stand back. Give him some air. Some of you men pick him up and carry him into that room."

Several men picked Jim up and carried him inside a small room in one of the buildings. I followed them in and sat in a corner. I watched them lay Jim on a small bed.

"Bring me some water and some towels," Dr. Pollard said.

"What's happened to Jim?" Juana asked as she and Gertrudis ran into the room.

"He's very sick," Dr. Pollard said. Someone brought a bowl of water and some towels. Dr. Pollard began to wash the dirt from Jim's face.

"All right, everyone," Colonel Travis said. "Time to get back to your posts. The enemy might attack any time."

The men left the room. Colonel Travis walked over to Dr. Pollard.

"I need to write some letters. I'll check on him later."

Dr. Pollard nodded and continued to wash Jim's face. I moved over by the bed. Travis patted me on the head as he left. Juana knelt next to Jim's bed. She looked up at Dr. Pollard.

"Let me do that. You have other people to look after."

Dr. Pollard handed her the towel. "Keep washing his face. We need to keep him cool. He has a fever. I'll check on him later. I'll see if there's any medicine I can give him."

Dr. Pollard walked out of the room. Juana and Gertrudis were taking good care of Jim so I walked outside. Men were looking over the walls at the enemy army. The enemy cannons fired every now and then. They caused some damage, but no one was injured. I saw Colonel Travis walk out of his room and hand a letter to a man on horseback. Travis said something to the man. The man nodded, then turned his horse and rode out of the gate. The gates closed after the messenger rode off.

Although there were people everywhere, I felt alone as I walked around the old mission. I was worried about Jim. I knew he had more than a cold. I walked by the chapel where the women and children were staying. Susannah Dickinson walked out holding her baby. She stared across the courtyard at her husband firing a cannon at the enemy. She sat down and leaned against the chapel wall. I sat next to her. She put a hand on my head. We sat there a long time, neither of us moving. Susannah watched her husband while I thought about Jim. The baby started to cry. Susannah patted my head, stood up and walked back into the chapel.

I trotted over to Jim's room. As my eyes adjusted to the dark room, I saw Jim sitting up in bed. Juana was feeding him some soup. I ran over to the bed and stood on my back legs with my front legs on Jim's bed.

Gertrudis tried to push me away. "Go on, Gator. Jim needs to eat and rest."

Jim shook his head. "Leave him alone, Gertrudis. We've been friends for a long time. I'm happy to see him."

Jim put his hand on my head. His touch was weak. Juana tried to give Jim some soup. She spilled some and the hot soup fell on my nose. I yelped and jumped back. Jim laughed until he began to cough. He patted the bed beside where he was lying.

"Come here, boy. That was the funniest thing I've seen in a while. You always could make me laugh."

I put my head on the bed next to Jim. He laid his hand on me and scratched between my ears. Outside the cannons were shooting and the men were yelling, but in that small room with Jim scratching my ears, I felt a strange peace.

Chapter Twenty-three

JIM GREW WEAKER WITH EACH PASSING DAY. Juana and Gertrudis stayed with him and did the best they could to make him feel better, but there was not much they could do. One day Dr. Pollard stopped by. He checked Jim then walked outside with Juana. I followed them into the courtyard.

"You're doing a good job," Dr. Pollard said.

Juana's eyes filled with tears. "He's not getting any better. Sometimes he feels stronger, but then he begins to cough and he becomes very sick. What's wrong with him, Doctor?"

Dr. Pollard took off his hat and ran his fingers through his hair.

"I don't know for sure. He has tuberculosis or pneumonia, or typhoid or all of them. I just call it consumption. You're doing all you can for him. Just keep him comfortable and try to get him to eat something. I better go. I have some sick men over in the next room I need to check on."

Juana watched him walk away, then went back into the little room. Gertrudis was wiping Jim's forehead with a wet cloth. Juana sat in a chair next to the bed. Jim was sleeping.

"Gertrudis, why don't you go outside for awhile? I'll stay with Jim."

Gertrudis put down her cloth. "All right. It's getting cold. I'll find some wood for the fire."

She put her shawl around her shoulders and walked outside. Suddenly there was a lot of shooting going on. I ran outside and saw men firing from the wall. Davy Crockett was walking behind the men, patting them on the back and encouraging them. Finally the firing stopped. The men on the wall cheered. I heard one of them say, "Look at them run."

I walked back into the room. Jim was sitting up, asking Juana what was happening. She told Jim she didn't know. At that moment Davy Crockett walked through the door. He took off his cap and stood next to the bed.

"How are you doing, Jim?"

Jim smiled weakly at Davy. "Why, I'm just fine, Davy. Pretty soon I'll be wrestling alligators again. What was all the shooting about?"

"The enemy made a brief attack. I think they just wanted to see how strong we were. We drove them off, but those little shacks just outside the walls give them good cover."

Jim coughed then looked up at Davy. "You need to burn them down. I bet there are some enemy soldiers in them right now. They'll be a big problem if you leave them."

"That's what I was thinking, Jim. I told Travis to let me take some men out there and burn them down. We're going in a few minutes. I just wanted to check on you."

Jim reached his hand toward Davy. "Thank you. I'll be all right. Juana and Gator are taking good care of me. Before long I'll be right out there with you again."

I walked beside Davy as he walked into the courtyard. Colonel Travis and a group of men were waiting for him. The men held torches.

"We're ready, Davy," Colonel Travis said. "I'll have the men on the north wall shoot to draw the enemy's attention away from you. Get those shacks to burning as soon as you can, then hurry back."

Davy nodded and led his men to a small gate. I walked back to Jim's room and sat in the doorway. Soon the men on the wall began to fire. The small gate was opened and Davy and his men ran outside the Alamo. Soon I saw smoke rising from the shacks. I heard firing coming from the direction of the burning shacks. Suddenly the small gate opened and Davy and his men ran through the gate and fell to the ground. They were breathing heavily. Before long the men caught their breath and stood up. I saw Davy walking toward Jim's room. He patted me on the head as he walked past. Jim smiled when he saw Davy walk in.

"Well, Davy. Sounded like you stirred up quite a hornets' nest."

Davy shook his head. "It seems they didn't want to move out. You were right, Jim. There were enemy soldiers hiding in those shacks. I guess they're going to have to find a new place to live now."

There was a knock on the door. Colonel Travis and Juan Seguin walked into the room.

"Hello," Jim said. "We're getting enough people in here to have a party. What's going on, Travis?"

"Jim, as you know, we need more men. I've sent out messengers requesting more men, but I haven't heard from any of them. I want Juan to take another message. He doesn't want to go. I know you are good friends, so I was hoping you could talk him into going."

"Why don't you want to go, Juan?" Jim asked.

"Jim, I have many friends here. I can't go and leave them. Some of these men followed me here. What would they think if they saw me ride away? There are other men who could carry the message."

"Juan, I told you why I want you to go," Travis said. "You are familiar with the country. You speak Spanish. You have the best chance to get the message through the enemy lines. After you see General Houston, you can bring me his answer. It's important that we get more men. I think you're the one to bring them back to us."

"He's right, Juan," Jim said. "No one will think badly about you. We'll look forward to you coming back with more men."

Juan sighed. "All right. I'll go, but I need to borrow your horse, Jim. Mine's lame."

"Sure, Juan. I'll be glad to let you use him. Good luck."

Juan shook Jim's hand. "I'll be back soon."

The men left the room. In a little while the gate opened and we listened to the sound of the horse's feet pounding on the road. Soon the hoof beats faded away. I lay down in a corner of the room. The enemy cannons continued to pound the walls. I hoped Juan would bring more men soon.

Chapter Twenty-four

THE WEATHER WAS COLDER NOW. The men standing on the walls blew on their hands and lit small fires to keep warm. I stayed in the room most of the time. I lay next to the fire and tried to keep warm. Juana and Gertrudis took turns watching Jim. They fed him soup and would always bring me a bone or some meat scraps. The enemy cannons fired all the time. They damaged some of the walls, but none of the men had been hurt. Colonel Travis sent out more messengers. So far none of the messengers had come back, so we did not know if anybody was coming to join us.

One night the door to the room opened. Davy Crockett walked into the room. He walked over to Jim's bed and smiled down at him.

"How do you feel, Jim?" he asked.

"I feel pretty good right now. I'm tired of laying in this bed."

"Well then, I have a treat for you." He motioned to the door and four men walked in. They each picked up a corner of the bed and started to carry it outside.

Juana ran and stood in front of the door. "What are you doing?" she asked.

Davy laughed. "John MacGregor and I have a bet about who can play the loudest. He has his bagpipes and I have my fiddle. I thought Jim would like to judge the contest."

Juana shook her head. "I don't think Jim should be outside in this cold weather."

"We have some extra blankets outside. We'll keep him warm," Davy told her.

"It's all right, Juana. I want to go outside. I'll be fine. It'll be fun to judge the contest."

Juana stood aside as the men carried Jim outside. I walked next to her as we followed them. A group of men was gathered around a fire in the courtyard. Some of the women had come out of the chapel and were watching. I saw Colonel Travis come out of his room and walk over to the group. The men placed Jim down close to the fire. Davy Crockett stepped in front of the men and raised his hand.

"Tonight we're going to have a contest. I have my fiddle and John MacGregor has his bagpipes. The contest is to see who can play the loudest. The judge of the contest is Jim Bowie."

The men cheered and clapped. Davy picked up his fiddle and nodded to John MacGregor. The men began to play. The noise sounded like cats fighting in a bag. The men began to cheer and called for the musicians to play louder. Suddenly it was possible to hear a tune coming from the noise. Davy and MacGregor began to play a song. The men clapped their hands and stomped their feet in time to the song. A few of the men walked over to the women who were watching and began to dance. Soon everyone was laughing and yelling. It seemed that they were having the best time of their lives. The loud music drowned out the sound of the cannons. Jim was laughing and shouting along with the others. At last the music ended. The people cheered and clapped for several minutes.

"We want more," the people yelled.

Davy and MacGregor played several more songs. More people came to watch and listen. Everyone seemed to forget where they were. They seemed not to care that there was an enemy army surrounding them and that the enemy cannons were tearing down the walls to their fort. At last the music stopped. Davy and MacGregor walked over and stood next to Jim's bed.

"All right, Jim," Davy said. "It's time for you to choose. Who's the winner?"

Jim raised himself onto his elbows. He smiled as he looked around at the men. They were watching him as if he were going to make a great announcement. Finally he shook his head.

"I tell you, that was the worst bunch of noise I have ever heard. I really can't tell who was loudest. You were both loud. I think the only thing to do is to have another contest later. Maybe I can pick a winner then."

Everybody cheered and clapped in agreement with Jim's announcement. Colonel Travis walked to the front of the group.

"Men. It's time to get back to your posts."

The men turned and walked toward the walls. The women returned to the chapel. Four men started to pick up Jim's bed.

"Wait a minute," he said. He sniffed the night air. He looked up at the moon that was being covered by a cloud. "It feels so good to be out here. That room is so small. It's good to see the sky and smell the fresh air. I wish I could stay out here."

Jim began to cough and Juana called to the men. "Hurry. Get him back inside. He's getting chilled."

The men picked up the bed and carried it into the room, then left to go back to their posts. As Davy was leaving, Jim called to him.

"Thank you, Davy. I enjoyed that."

Davy smiled back at him. "We'll do it again, Jim."

As Jim watched Davy walk out of the room, I thought I saw a tear roll down Jim's cheek. He closed his eyes and was soon sleeping. I curled up in front of the fire. I sure hoped that more men would be here soon.

Chapter
Twenty-five

AS THE DAYS PASSED, ALL ANYONE TALKED ABOUT was when reinforcements would arrive. Sentries on the wall scanned the horizon for a sign that men were coming to join us. Jim drifted in and out of consciousness. When he felt good, men would carry him outdoors and he would talk to the defenders. It raised the spirits of the tired men to talk to Jim, and Jim felt better outside. When the fever rose, he turned on his bed while Juana and Gertrudis wiped the sweat from his face. At those times I would walk outside. I could not stand to see my friend suffer like that.

One evening I was lying by the fire when I heard a sentry shout.

"Riders coming."

I ran outside to see what was happening. Men raced to the walls, preparing to fight off an attack. Someone fired a shot, then a voice from outside the walls cried out. "Don't shoot. We're Texans."

The front gate opened and a group of men rode into the courtyard. The defenders gathered around the new-comers as they dismounted. Colonel Travis ran up to the leader. I recognized him as John Smith. Travis had sent him from the Alamo as a messenger early in the battle.

"John," Travis said as he grabbed the scout's hand. "I'm glad to see you. How many men have you brought us?"

Smith looked at the group of men who had followed him into the Alamo.

"Here are thirty-two men. I guess these are all the able-bodied men in Gonzales."

Disappointment crossed Travis's face. He tried to hide it as he welcomed the new men.

"We're glad to have you join us. Captain Dickinson will show you where your positions will be."

Davy Crockett walked in front of the group. "I say let's give a cheer for the brave men from Gonzales. We welcome you to our little army."

The defenders cheered for the new men. Crockett thought for a moment then, spoke again. "You men can help us out with a little problem we have. John Mac-Gregor and I cannot decide who can play the loudest. So when you get settled in, I'll get my fiddle and John will get his bagpipes and we'll let you be the judges."

As the men walked away, Travis spoke to John Smith.

"Do you have any news of Colonel Fannin?"

Smith shook his head. "I thought he would be here. We thought we would meet him on the way, but we saw no sign of him. We thought he had come on ahead of us."

Travis tried to smile. "Well, maybe he's not far behind. If you could get through the enemy lines so easily, surely Colonel Fannin with his men can too."

Smith went to join his men, and Colonel Travis walked to his quarters. I followed Davy Crockett as he entered Jim's room. Jim was sitting up in his bed.

"What's all the noise about, Davy?"

"Thirty-two men from Gonzales just rode in."

"Thirty-two men?" Jim shook his head. "We need a lot more than that."

"I know we do, Jim," Davy said. "But thirty-two is a start. I'm sure many more will be here soon."

Jim lay back on his bed. He stared at the ceiling for several minutes.

"I should have done what Houston told me and blown up this place," he said.

Davy walked over and put his hand on Jim's shoulder.

"No, Jim. This place is important. What we do here is important. We're giving time to Texas so she can survive."

Jim smiled up at Davy. "You're right. I just wish I could be of more help. I hate lying here in this bed."

"I know you do, Jim. But the men feel better just knowing that Jim Bowie is with them. They are proud to be fighting with you."

"Davy, you know just what to say. Pull up a chair and stay awhile."

Davy shook his head. "I can't right now, Jim. I promised those Gonzales boys I would let them judge a contest between John MacGregor and me. It seems that the judge we had before had a hard time making a decision."

Jim laughed and then began to cough. He waved to Davy.

"Go on. I hope those new men don't leave when they hear you play. Come back when you have time."

"I'll come back later."

He turned and walked outside. I walked over and curled up next to the fireplace. The fire had burned down, but it was still warm. Soon I heard the sound of the fiddle and bagpipes. Men were cheering and laughing as the music got louder. I looked over at Jim. He was smiling as he stared at the ceiling. Soon he closed his eyes and went to sleep. I lay there listening to the music. I hoped that somewhere outside the walls of the Alamo, Colonel Fannin could hear the music and was on his way to join us.

Chapter
Twenty-six

THE AIR WAS NOT AS COLD TODAY. Jim scratched my ears as I sat by his bed. I reached up and licked his hand.

"Well, Gator," he said. "When we get out of here, we need to go on a long hunting trip. Maybe go wrestle some alligators. What do you think?"

Wrestling alligators did not sound like fun, but I was glad to hear Jim talk about doing something after we left the Alamo. Juana and Gertrudis were not in the room. I liked it when it was just Jim and me. It made it seem like the old days. Back before Jim got so sick. Suddenly I heard someone yell.

"Rider coming in. Open the gates."

I ran to the door and looked out. The gates opened

and a rider raced his horse into the courtyard. As he leaped from the horse, I recognized James Bonham, one of Colonel Travis's messengers. Bonham went straight to Colonel Travis's room. The men stood outside the closed door and waited to hear the news that Bonham had brought. After several minutes, Colonel Travis opened the door. His face was grim. He called to the men.

"Assemble in the courtyard. I have news I need to share with you."

The men walked into the courtyard and stood in a line. Davy and several men came into Jim's room.

"Colonel Travis is going to talk to us. Do you feel like listening?" he asked.

"I sure do," Jim replied.

The men picked up Jim's bed and carried him outside. They set the bed down on the end of the line. I sat next to Jim. I looked down the line of men waiting for Travis. They were tired and dirty, but there was a look in their eyes that said they were far from beaten. At last Colonel Travis and James Bonham came outside. Bonham walked over and stood in line with the others while Travis walked to the center of the line and faced the men.

"Men, James Bonham has brought us bad news. Colonel Fannin is not coming. Nor does he know of any other groups marching to reinforce us."

A murmur rose from the men. Travis raised his hand.

"As you know, I have sent out many messengers requesting reinforcements. It seems that all the requests are not going to be answered. So the question now is, what do we do? It's not a question for me. I'll stay and fight here as long as I can. Every day we keep Santa Anna here is another day that the rest of Texas has to build up its army to defeat him. But I can ask you to do no more. You have done all that can be expected of you. If any of you wants to try and escape through the enemy lines, you may do so. There can be no blame attached to you for such an attempt. But if you want to stay here with me and fight for Texas independence, then I will thank you and Texas will thank you."

Travis drew his sword. He walked to the end of the row of men and traced a line in the dirt from one end of the row to the other. He replaced his sword and walked back to the center of the line.

"All those who wish to stay with me and fight for Texas independence… cross the line."

For a moment no one moved. Each man was thinking about what Travis was asking them to do. He was asking them not to fight for Texas independence, but to die for it. Finally I saw a young man step out of the ranks and cross the line. Then another. And then another. Soon the entire line was moving toward Colonel Travis. Soon only Jim and one other man were left. I saw Jim struggle to one elbow' then sink back down onto his bed. I heard him call out to the men on the other side of the line.

"Boys, I would dearly like to join you, but it seems I can't get up. I would appreciate it if some of you could give me a hand in coming over to your side."

Several men rushed to Jim's bed. They lifted him up and carried him across the line. The men cheered as Jim was placed down next to Travis. I followed Jim and sat next to his bed. All the men stared at the man standing on the other side of the line. His name was Louis Moses

Rose. Jim knew him. Jim called over to him.

"You seem not to be willing to stay with us, Rose."

Rose shook his head. "No. I don't believe I'm willing to stay."

Davy Crockett stepped forward and said. "You might as well come over to us. You can't get away."

Rose shook his head. "No. I'll try." He looked at his friends and then looked at the wall. "I've done much worse than to climb that wall."

We watched as Rose climbed to the top of the wall. He looked back at us and waved. He jumped to the other side and vanished into the darkness. Travis turned to the men.

"I thank you. And Texas thanks you. Now we had better get back to our posts."

The men walked away. Each was lost in his own thoughts. Some of the men carried Jim into his room. I sat next to the bed. Davy Crockett walked into the room. He came over and laid two pistols next to Jim.

"I think you'll need these when the attack comes," he said.

Jim nodded. "Thanks. Would you hand me my knife? I feel better when I have it nearby."

Davy picked up the knife and handed it to Jim. "I don't think it'll be long until the final attack comes."

Jim nodded. "I think you're right." Jim reached out his hand to Davy. "Thanks for all you've done, Davy. Good luck to you."

Davy took his hand. "Thank you, Jim. Good luck to you." Davy walked outside.

Jim looked over at Gertrudis and Juana. "I want you

to go and stay with the women."

"Who'll take care of you if we do?" Juana asked.

"I'm fine right now. You'll be safer there. Besides, I have Gator. He can watch out for me. Now go on. I need to get some rest."

The two women walked out into the dark courtyard. I watched them walk toward the Alamo chapel. Jim lay on his bed and was soon asleep. I curled up in a corner of the room. I noticed that the enemy cannon was not firing. I was glad. Maybe I could get some sleep tonight.

Chapter
Twenty-seven

IT WAS THE BEST SLEEP I HAD HAD IN WEEKS. I dreamed I
was running through a field of tall blue flowers, chasing
rabbits. The wind blowing through my ears felt good. I
saw Jim running behind me, laughing and yelling. It was
like old times.

The sound of a cannonball crashing into the wall of
the Alamo woke me from my dream. I heard someone
shout.

"Here they come!"

I ran to the door and looked out into the courtyard. I
saw Colonel Travis running from his room carrying his
shotgun. He ran toward the north wall, shouting, "Don't
surrender, boys."

Jim Bowie

I saw men stumbling from the rooms where they had been sleeping. They rubbed their eyes as they ran toward their positions on the walls. Davy Crockett and his men were firing at the advancing enemy. I heard the enemy band playing loud music, and then the roar of the cannons and the firing of the muskets drowned the music out.

I turned and saw that Jim had raised himself into a sitting position on the bed. He braced his back against the wall and held a pistol in each hand. His knife lay across his lap. He looked at me and gave me a small smile.

"Well, Gator. Looks like we're in for it now."

I turned back toward the battle. I saw Colonel Travis lying at the foot of the north wall. His shotgun lay next to him. All around the Alamo men were firing at the advancing enemy. Sometimes I would see the top of a ladder rest against the wall. Then a Texan would push it off and I could hear yells as the enemy fell to the ground. The firing slowed for a moment. I heard someone yell.

"They're running!"

Shortly I heard someone else yell.

"Here they come again!"

The firing seemed louder this time. Men were yelling as they fired into the advancing enemy. I had never heard noise like this before in my life. I saw some Texans fall from the walls. Some men ran out of ammunition, and I watched them search everywhere for more.

I saw the first of the enemy soldiers climb inside the Alamo on the north wall. Texans rushed to meet them and they fought hand-to-hand in the thickening gunsmoke that was beginning to cover the area. More and more enemy soldiers climbed over the wall. The outnumbered

111

Texans were gradually forced back. In a short period of time, the enemy controlled the north wall.

Other Texans turned to face the new enemy threat. As they turned from their places, more enemy troops climbed the walls and they were inside the Alamo. I saw some enemy soldiers run to the gate. Despite the efforts of a few defenders, the gate was opened and the enemy army stormed through. Some of the Texans jumped from the walls and raced to the rooms where they had prepared their defenses. They began to fire on the enemy soldiers from these new positions. I saw the enemy soldiers attacking the rooms. They turned the Texans' cannons around and fired them into the rooms. I knew it was only a matter of time until they found Jim.

I walked over to the bed and lay down next to Jim. We listened to the sound of the battle. We could see figures running by the door. We heard men yelling as they fought each other. Suddenly I saw an enemy soldier stick his head into the room. He saw Jim lying on the bed. He yelled something, and soon other soldiers appeared in the doorway. They started to come into the room. I heard the sound of Jim's guns as he fired at the advancing soldiers. He dropped his guns to the floor and picked up his knife.

I ran toward the first soldier. My teeth were bared, and I growled as I leaped at him. He saw me coming and swung his rifle. The rifle hit me in the side and I hit the floor and rolled into a corner. I lay there stunned for a moment. When I recovered I saw the enemy soldiers standing around Jim's bed. I knew my best friend was gone.

I ran from the room. One of the soldiers saw me and

stuck his bayonet toward me. I felt the sharp blade slice down my leg. I yelped but kept running. As I ran through the courtyard, I saw the Texans still fighting. Davy Crockett and his men were fighting their way toward the Alamo chapel. Davy was leading the way, swinging his rifle at the advancing enemy. The gate was full of enemy troops rushing into the Alamo. I saw a cannon position in the stockade area where Davy and his men had been fighting. I ran to the cannon and jumped on top of it. The cannon was hot from firing, and it burned my feet as I jumped over the fence and landed on the outside of the Alamo. I ran as fast as I could. I did not know where I was going, but I knew I had to get out of that place.

Soon I came to the top of a small hill. I stopped to catch my breath. I looked back toward the battle. The firing had nearly stopped. I watched as more enemy troops entered the Alamo. I saw some enemy soldiers lower the flag that had been flying over the Alamo and raise their own flag. As I stood there, I felt sadder than I had ever felt in my life. The one person in this world I loved more than any other was gone.

The sun was starting to come up, but the moon was still visible in the sky. I raised my face toward the moon and howled as long and as loud as I could. When I could howl no more, I turned and limped away from the Alamo.

Chapter
Twenty-eight

THE OLD DOG LOOKED DOWN AT THE young puppies. They were both asleep. Princess lay with her front paw touching the old dog's leg. Butch moved his feet and growled as he chased rabbits in his dream. The old dog stretched and yawned. He was ready for a nap too.

A small dust devil blew across the yard. It picked up leaves and deposited them not far from where the old dog lay. He watched the dust devil pass out of the yard and disappear in the distance. The water dish looked inviting, but the old dog did not want to get up and walk over to it.

His leg ached where the bayonet had cut him so many years ago. It seemed now that it had all been a dream. He missed Jim. Many times during the past years he had thought that he heard Jim calling him. He would run toward the sound, but when he got there it would only be the wind.

The old dog had been found by a young couple who had adopted him. They were nice to him and he enjoyed being part of their family, but they could not replace Jim.

The young couple had a dog, and the old dog came to like her. They had had some puppies, and later Princess and Butch had come along. He loved the little puppies and enjoyed telling them stories of when he was young. He wanted them to know about his great friend, Jim Bowie. He wanted them to remember what Jim and the others had done to win Texas independence. To remember the sacrifices they had made so that new Texans could enjoy the freedoms they now had. He remembered. He would always remember, not only the Alamo, but also the men who had defended it. Men like William Travis, Davy Crockett, and his great friend, Jim Bowie.

The old dog looked around. The shade was disappearing. If he was going to take a nap, he needed to take one soon. He looked up and watched a passing cloud cover the sun. The old dog placed his head on his paws and closed his eyes. Soon all was still in the yard.

The End